By Mark Bonito

Vanlife Eats

Recipes
Inspired by Travel & Adventure

Edited By Sophie Why

Written & photographed by Mark Bonito
Edited by Sophie Why

This book is a celebration of street food from around the world, adapted for life on the road or for any tiny kitchen . If you love the recipes, share your creations and tag us on social media—we'd love to see what you're cooking!

🌍 Website: www.vanlifeeats.com
Instagram: @vanlife_eats
YouTube: @VanlifeEats
Facebook: groups/vanlifeeats
TikTok: @vanlifeeats

For exclusive recipes, live cooking lessons, and more, visit:
🔗 **www.vanlifeeats.com/vip**

First edition, printed in England, United Kingdom
ISBN: 978-1-0683795-0-5

Meet Mark

Hey, I'm Mark, and I live and breathe food, travel, and adventure. I'm a passionate cook, blogger, food writer, author, and all-around culinary explorer.

My journey with food started from the moment I could reach a wooden spoon, growing up in an English/Italian family where the kitchen was the heart of both homes. My mother was always cooking fresh home-cooked English meals whilst my Nonna and Aunties were always in the kitchen cooking authentic Italian food. My Italian family are from the breathtaking Amalfi Coast, specifically the charming village of Minori, where food has always been a way of life.

Minori is legendary for Italian culinary tradition, a place where some of the greatest chefs, including Jamie Oliver, have come to learn the true art of Italian cooking. My family has always been deeply embedded in this world, with my grandfather working as a chef alongside Gennaro Contaldo, Jamie's mentor and a family friend. My relative, Ursula Ferrigno, is a renowned Italian chef and author, carrying forward the traditions of authentic Italian cuisine. To say ragu runs in my veins would be an understatement!

But my love of food isn't just about perfecting nonna's recipes—it's about discovering flavors from all corners of the world. That passion led me to embrace vanlife, converting a campervan into a mobile kitchen and setting off on a mission to explore and share the diverse street food cultures of the world. My journey is all about pushing the boundaries of what's possible in a tiny kitchen.

This mission became Vanlife Eats—a platform dedicated to showing people that incredible meals aren't reserved for those with restaurant-grade kitchens. Whether you're cooking in a campervan, a boat, or a tiny apartment, I teach people how to make mouthwatering dishes with minimal equipment and maximum flavour.
My audience isn't just vanlifers but anyone who embraces the adventure of cooking in unconventional spaces.

I also run my own food festival, the Vanlife Eats Festival, which sells out year after year. My work has taken me to some of the biggest food events in the UK, where I don't just show up—I bring my love of food to life with high-energy cookery demos, workshops, and engaging storytelling about the incredible dishes I've encountered on my travels as well as that "movie scene" Italian lifestyle I was born into.

And if that wasn't enough, I've taken my knowledge and passion and turned it into the Vanlife Eats Cookery School, where I teach people how to cook like a pro in any space. This is my first cookbook, with a second pasta-focused book hot on its heels.

So, whether you catch me at an event, tune into my latest cooking demo, or flick through one of my recipes, one thing's for sure—I'm here to prove that great food has no boundaries. Adventure starts in the kitchen, and I'll be taking your tastebuds on a tour around the world!

Travel Cooking Essentials for Motorhomes and Campervans

When I first started vanlife, it seemed obvious to go for lightweight, stackable cookware. It seemed perfect on paper, but after a few months of full-time cooking, the pans tarnished, warped, and left me frustrated. I then went to the other extreme, investing in professional-grade cookware that was fantastic for a stationary kitchen but far too heavy and bulky for a campervan.

After years of trial and error, I've settled on a middle ground: durable, high-quality, and compact gear that works hard without weighing me (or my van) down. Space in the van cupboards is precious, and only products that are multi-use, space-saving, but without any issues regarding durability are worthy.

Here's everything you need to know about setting up your tiny kitchen for successful cooking on the road.

Multi-Functional Cookware
In a small kitchen, every item needs to pull its weight. That's why I highly recommend investing in multi-functional cookware. My favourite pan is an all-in-one frying pan, saucepan, oven dish, and even a steamer, thanks to its clever design and removable handle. It's perfect for whipping up anything from a stir-fry to baked pasta, all without cluttering your cupboards.

I've found RidgeMonkey products to be incredibly good. Their compact, stackable kitchenware is built for tiny kitchens, such as for vanlife, and designed to last, making it ideal for everything from casual cooks to full-time foodies. We even bake brownies in a RidgeMonkey sandwich toaster!

Knives
A sharp, high-quality chef's knife is non-negotiable. A good knife makes prep faster, safer, and far more enjoyable. Keep it sharp and well-maintained, and it will serve you for years. Many brands offer protective sheaths for storage, which are great for keeping your knife safe (and your fingers, too) in a moving vehicle.

I have spent a lot of money over the years on knives, but I have come to the conclusion that as long as it is a well-kept knife, then it is going to serve you well. From a well-forged high-priced knife to a supermarket brand, you will still get excellent results so long as the knife is sharp and straight.

Compact and Clever Gadgets
Space is a premium in any campervan, so compact tools are essential:

- Collapsible bowls: These save loads of space and are perfect for everything from washing veggies to mixing dough.
- Manual blender: My absolute favourite kitchen essential! It's perfect for chopping onions (tear-free!), dicing garlic, or making a quick salsa without any mess or electricity.
- Food-grade blow torch: This nifty gadget is perfect for adding a golden, crispy finish to dishes like crème brûlée or roasted veggies. It's small, portable, and surprisingly versatile.

For Those Without an Oven
No oven? No problem! The Omnia stovetop oven is a must-have for any campervan equipped only with a stovetop hob. It's brilliant for baking bread, roast potatoes, chips, cakes, or even casseroles right on your hob. Lightweight and easy to store, it opens up so many cooking possibilities without taking up too much room. This clever little gadget has completely changed how I cook on the road. That's right, folks, pizza is back on the menu!

Staying Clean, Tidy, and Organised While Cooking
One of the best ways to keep your tiny kitchen functional is by staying organised. A simple tray to catch peelings and spills is a lifesaver when it comes to cleaning up. Whether you're peeling potatoes or flouring a surface for rolling dough, a tray keeps mess contained and makes cleanup quick and easy.

A Well Stocked Spice and Herb Rack
Turning a simple chicken and rice dish into something magical—whether it's Asian, Italian, or Moroccan—comes down to the sprinkle of the right herbs and spices. While I'm all for the convenience of pre-mixed spice blends, there's something undeniably satisfying about crafting your own unique flavour combinations.

Trust me, having a full collection of herbs and spices in a campervan can quickly become a game of Tetris. Space is precious, and those little jars have a way of taking over. That's why I highly recommend modular spice racks or compact containers that make storage more manageable.

Here's my list of essential herbs and spices to keep your dishes flavour-packed and versatile:

- Paprika (smoked) – Adds depth to everything from stews to roasted veggies.
- Cumin – Perfect for Mexican, Indian, or Middle Eastern dishes.
- Chilli Flakes – For when you need just a touch of heat.
- Oregano – A must for Italian sauces, marinades, and more.
- Turmeric – Great for colour and a subtle earthiness in curries and rice dishes.
- Ground Cinnamon – Not just for desserts—it's a secret weapon for savoury Moroccan recipes.
- Coriander (Ground) – Essential for curries and spice blends.
- Salt and Pepper – Because no dish should ever go without the basics.

Fresh Herbs
Whilst dried herbs have their place in countless recipes, there's something undeniably special about fresh herbs. They add vibrancy, fragrance, and a burst of freshness to your dishes, especially when sprinkled on right at the end of cooking. Fresh herbs enhance the flavour and transform your meal into something that feels alive and full of character.

Here are my essential fresh herbs:

- Parsley – Versatile and bright, parsley adds a fresh finish to soups, stews, and salads. It's also perfect for garnishing everything from pasta to grilled fish.
- Coriander (Cilantro) – The hero of curries, stir-fries, and Mexican dishes. Its citrusy zing lifts the entire dish.
- Basil – A classic for Italian dishes, especially fresh tomato sauces, Caprese salads, or pesto. The sweet aroma is irresistible.
- Mint – Refreshing and cooling, mint is a game-changer in drinks, desserts, and even savoury dishes like lamb or couscous.
- Dill – Delicate and aromatic, dill pairs beautifully with fish, potatoes, and creamy dressings.
- Rosemary – While also great dried, fresh rosemary's intense aroma is unbeatable for roasting meats, vegetables, or potatoes.
- Thyme – Perfect for slow-cooked dishes like stews, roasts, and sauces. Its earthy flavour blends seamlessly into hearty meals.
- Chives – Great for adding a subtle onion flavour without overpowering a dish. Sprinkle them over eggs, potatoes, or soups for a final touch.

Here's a quick recap of my must-have items for cooking in a campervan:

- Multi-functional cookware.
- RidgeMonkey stackable kitchenware for compact storage.
- A sharp chef's knife with a protective sheath.
- Collapsible bowls for space-saving versatility.
- A manual blender for mess-free chopping and quick prep.
- A food-grade blow torch for finishing dishes like a pro.
- Omnia stove top oven for those without a built-in oven.
- A tray to catch peelings and spills, keeping the workspace tidy.
- A fully loaded herb and spice rack to add flavour from around the world.
- Fresh herbs to bring your dish to life and add vibrancy.

With these essentials in your campervan kitchen, you'll be ready to cook up everything from simple one-pot meals to adventurous street food dishes from around the world, all while keeping your setup practical, organised, and compact. If you're a full-time vanlifer or a weekend road tripper, these essentials will transform your tiny kitchen into a space where anything is possible and big flavours come to life.

Frying in a Campervan

Frying in a campervan might sound like a disaster in the making. I get it, and I once felt the same. There's the fear of greasy food, lingering cooking smells, or the dreaded oil splatter on your brand-new worktop. But here's what I discovered: frying in a campervan is not nearly as scary as it seems. With a few tricks, some prep, and a touch of adventure, you can pull off fried chicken, crispy calamari, and so many street food-inspired dishes.

Ventilation - It's All About the Airflow

No one wants to sleep in a van that smells like last night's fish fest. Getting the ventilation right is crucial. A common mistake I often see people make is to open all the windows in the van. This causes chaos in the airflow, and the smells go around in circles whilst kissing every nook and cranny of your interior. My go-to trick? Set the fan to extraction mode and crack open just one window. If you have a fan at the front and rear, then set the front to extract and the rear to blow air in. This creates a concentrated cross-flow that whisks the smells right out of your van. And yes, it works! Even if you're making something as fragrant as garlic prawns.

I'll never forget the day I made a fish pie in the van. Not only did I ruin a silicone liner for our Omnia oven, but I didn't ventilate the van properly, and man did it stink out the van! Lesson learned: always double-check ventilation!

Minimal Oil

One of the biggest myths about frying is that you need a pool of oil. You don't. I keep it simple: a light coating of the bottom of the pan with rapeseed oil is often all I need. It has a high smoke point, so it's perfect for frying without setting off the smoke alarm. I steer clear of deep frying with olive oil. Olive oil burns easily and the flavor can taint your food.

Disposing of Oil

This is where vanlife ingenuity shines and disposing of used oil needs to be done responsibly and safely.

1. Save kitchen roll scraps.
2. Soak up the oil with the kitchen roll.
3. Toss the oily paper into a reused container, like an old yogurt pot, before binning it.

It's eco-conscious and keeps your grey water tank free of grease. Because trust me, cleaning an oil-clogged sink pipe in a campervan is no fun.

Be Well Prepared

Cooking in a tiny kitchen like that of a campervan has its challenges and if you're not prepared, it's chaos. When it comes to frying, I've learned to always have within arm's reach:

- A good, sturdy pan with the handle turned away to avoid knocking into it.
- Tongs: They just make it easier to move things around the pan in spitting oil.
- Kitchen roll: Not just for oil disposal—also handy for cleaning up those inevitable splatters as well as soaking up excess oil from fried food .
- A nearby plate lined with the kitchen roll: For placing the fried food.

And yes, organisation is key. Keep your work area clean and your tools within reach. Scrambling to find a plate while your prawns are turning golden is how meals end up burnt —or worse, on the floor.

Safety First

Cooking in a small space comes with its own risks, but a little caution goes a long way. My golden rule? Pan handles tucked in at all times. It's a simple habit, but it prevents accidental knocks that could send hot oil flying. Plus, in a campervan, you're usually working in tight quarters—every inch counts!

I also make sure to keep a fire extinguisher and a damp tea towel nearby. It's one of those things you hope you'll never need, but you'll be thankful to have if you do!

Greasy and Unhealthy Food?

It's a common misconception that all fried food is greasy and unhealthy. The key lies in getting the oil temperature just right. When the oil is hot enough, it instantly seals the outer coating of the food, locking in its natural juices. However, if the oil isn't hot enough, it won't form that quick seal, allowing the oil to soak into the food instead. This is what causes greasy, unappetising results.

A good rule of thumb? Heat the oil until it shimmers or reaches the temperature specified in your recipe—usually around 180–190°C (350–375°F) for most frying.

Takeaways for Campervan Frying

- Ventilation is key: Fan on extraction, one window open.
- Use minimal oil: Rapeseed oil is your best friend.
- Dispose of oil smartly: Soak it up with saved kitchen roll; use saved plastic containers to dispose of used oil.
- Stay organised: Utensils within reach, surfaces clean.
- Safety matters: Tuck pan handles in and have fire safety gear handy.

And above all, don't be afraid to experiment. Frying in a campervan is just like cooking anywhere else—it's about adapting, improvising, and enjoying the process. So go ahead, fry up some calamari or crispy fried chicken. Your van might smell like heaven for a while, but that's a price worth paying for good food from a street food-inspired menu.

Want to cook outside?

There are many products out there for outdoor cooking, but my personal favourite is the Cobb. It is portable and compact enough to store in a campervan's limited storage space, and it does just about everything!

How To Follow These Recipes

Cooking is such a personal endeavor, and there's so much of "you" that goes into making the final dish turn out the way you want it to. Every element plays a crucial role in the outcome, from the temperature of your oven to the thickness of your pans, and even the specific ingredients you choose can behave differently depending on where you are or what brand you're using. These little details can completely change cooking times and outcomes, leading to delightful surprises or unexpected mishaps. That's why I believe recipes should really just be seen as a guide—a flexible starting point for you to build upon and make uniquely your own.

Read the Recipe All the Way Through First
Now, let's delve into one of the most essential steps in the cooking process: reading the recipe all the way through before you start. Why is this so crucial? By taking the time to thoroughly read the entire recipe, you'll be able to spot any "surprise" instructions that might throw you off course, like needing to marinate your meat for 24 hours or realising you need a specific pan that you haven't seen since your last move. It also gives you a chance to familiarise yourself with the steps involved, the ingredients required, and the overall flow of the dish you're about to create. This preparation helps set you up for success and minimises the likelihood of running into unexpected hurdles once you're deep into the cooking process.

Prep Prep Prep
Honestly, what a huge difference it makes to get all your prep work done before you hit on step 1. Take the time to chop your onions, dice your peppers, and peel your potatoes ahead of time. This not only streamlines the cooking process but also allows you to focus on the actual cooking without the distraction of having to stop and prepare ingredients along the way.

I have a few small pots and bowls that I get out before I start any cooking session, especially if I am following a recipe. Having everything prepped and organised makes the entire experience more enjoyable and less chaotic. It gives you the freedom to immerse yourself in the cooking process, allowing your creativity to flow and the flavors to blossom without interruption. Remember, the more prepared you are, the more you can relax and enjoy the art of cooking!

Ask me!
If there is anything you are unsure about, I am all over social media so ask me and I will be happy to help. Better still join the Vanlife Eats VIP membership and learn some additional kitchen skills that help you feel your way through these recipe.

Good luck and I hope you enjoy this adventure!

Are you ready for a culinary adventure around the world?

Food Map

Asia

Africa

South America

North America

Europe

ASIA

In South Korea, there's a street food so dangerous it has a “chew or die” warning!
Sannakji—live baby octopus—is served wriggling on your plate, and if you don’t chew it properly, the suckers can latch onto your throat and choke you out like a tiny, slippery assassin.
So yeah, your food might actually fight back!

Curry Base Paste

This base is the foundation of 100's of different curry recipes. It uses the 4 pillar spices and veggies that will help you next level your curry game.

Prep: 5 minutes, Cook: 12 minutes, Servings: 4 portions

Equipment

Skillet or deep pan
Manual Blender (optional, but makes life easier)
Large Ice Cube Tray or small containers for freezing

Ingredients

2 medium red onions, finely chopped or blended
2 garlic cloves, minced or blended into a paste
1 tsp fresh ginger, minced or blended into a paste
4 tbsp passata
2 tbsp oil (ghee, coconut, or whatever's handy)
2 tbsp coriander powder
1 tbsp cumin powder
1 tsp turmeric
2 tsp red chilli powder

How to make it

Finely chop the onions–seriously, the finer, the better. If you're feeling lazy (or efficient), blitz them in a blender.
Do the same with your garlic and ginger–either chop super fine or blend with a splash of water into a paste.
If using fresh tomatoes instead of passata, chop them finely or blend until smooth.

Heat the oil in a decent pan (thin, cheap pans burn stuff –trust us). Ghee adds flavour, but any oil works.
Add the onion paste, garlic, and ginger. Stir well and cook for about 3-4 minutes until it starts to brown.

Toss in 1 tbsp coriander powder, ½ tbsp cumin powder, ½ tsp turmeric, and 1 tsp red chilli powder. Stir for about a minute, adding a splash of water if it looks too dry.
Stir in the passata and let it cook for 5 minutes until the mixture thickens into a lovely, fragrant paste.

Let the paste cool completely before dividing it into an ice cube tray or small containers.
Freeze until solid. When needed, pop out a cube or two and chuck it straight into your curry.

How to Use It
This is your shortcut to any curry–just add protein, veggies, or even chickpeas and you're golden. No more starting from scratch every time!

Paneer Popcorn

Crispy, golden nuggets of spiced paneer with a hint of chilli and a crunch that's utterly addictive. It's quick, fun, and packs a punch of flavour. Once you try it, you'll be frying up batches on every adventure.

Prep: 5 minutes, Cook: 7 minutes, Servings: 30 Bites

Equipment

Stove
Large pan
Tongs
Bowl
Maunal blender
Cutting board

Ingredients

For the Marinade:
200 grams paneer, cut into bite-sized cubes
1/4 tsp garam masala
1/4 tsp black pepper
1 tbsp yoghurt
Pinch of salt

For the Batter:
2 tbsp cornflour
1 tbsp all-purpose flour
1/4 tsp garam masala
Pinch of salt
Water, as needed to make a thick batter

For the Coating:
1 cup cornflakes, coarsely crushed
1/4 tsp tumeric
1/4 tsp red chilli flakes

For Frying:
Oil, for deep frying

How to make it

Marinate the Paneer:
In a bowl, combine paneer cubes with garam masala, black pepper, yoghurt, and salt.
Mix gently to ensure even coating.
Set aside for 10 minutes to allow flavors to meld.

Prepare the Batter:
In a separate bowl, mix together cornflour, all-purpose flour, garam masala, and salt.
Gradually add water to form a thick, smooth batter that can coat the back of a spoon.

Prepare the Coating:
Using your manual blender, blend up some cornflakes, chilli flakes, tumeric and a pinch of salt.

Coat the Paneer:
Dip each marinated paneer cube into the batter, ensuring it's fully coated.
Allow excess batter to drip off, then roll the paneer in the cornflake mixture, pressing lightly to adhere.

Fry the Paneer Popcorn:
Heat oil in a deep frying pan over medium heat.
Once the oil is hot, carefully add the coated paneer pieces in batches.

Fry until golden brown and crispy, turning occasionally for even cooking.

Use a slotted spoon to remove the paneer popcorn and drain on paper towels to remove excess oil.
Serve:

Serve hot with a nice chutney, coriander and yoghurt dip, tomato ketchup or your preferred dipping sauce.

Sticky Korean Chicken

Fried chicken at its best in my opinion! Sometimes I keep some without the sauce for a fried chicken fix! This sweet yet savoury and hot sauce is incredibly moreish. It's the real finger-lickin' good chicken!

Prep: 20 minutes, Cook: 20 mins Servings: 6 Chicken Thighs

Equipment

Large mixing bowl
Small saucepan
Deep frying pan or pot
Tongs
Wire rack or paper towels

Ingredients

For the Marinade
6 boneless chicken thighs
1 small knob of ginger, grated
2 garlic cloves, grated
1 tsp salt
1/2 tsp freshly ground black pepper

For the Sauce
1 tbsp peanut oil
3 tbsp gochujang (Korean chili paste)
3 tbsp tomato ketchup
1 ½ tbsp hot honey
3 garlic cloves, crushed
1 tbsp rice wine vinegar (or apple cider vinegar)
1 tsp soy sauce
2 tbsp water

For Frying
750ml (3 cups) frying oil of your choice
1 ½ cups (200g) plain flour
1 ½ cups (200g) cornstarch
2 eggs, lightly beaten
Spring onions and sesame seeds, for garnish

How to make it

Marinate the Chicken
Combine chicken pieces, ginger, garlic, salt, and pepper in a mixing bowl. Cover and refrigerate for at least 1 hour.

Make the Sauce
In a small saucepan, heat the peanut oil over medium heat. Add garlic and sauté for 2 minutes until fragrant. Stir in the gochujang, ketchup, hot honey, vinegar, soy sauce, and water. Simmer for 5 minutes until slightly thickened, then set aside.

Prepare the Oil
Heat your frying oil in a deep pan to 175°C (347°F).

Coat the Chicken
Add the eggs to the marinated chicken and mix to coat. In the same bowl, combine the flour and cornstarch. Coat each piece of chicken in the flour mixture, ensuring an even coating. Really get in with your hands.

First Fry
Working in batches, carefully place the chicken in the hot oil. Fry for 8-10 minutes until golden and crispy. Remove and drain on a wire rack or paper towels.

Second Fry
Increase the oil temperature to 190°C (375°F). Fry the chicken again for 5-6 minutes until extra crispy and cooked through. Drain as before.

Toss and Garnish
In a clean mixing bowl, toss the chicken with the prepared sauce. Sprinkle with sesame seeds and sliced spring onions.

Serve
Serve as they are for picking at or serve up with rice.

Honey Soy Chilli Glazed Salmon

This delicious glazed salmon, marinated in a mixture of honey, soy sauce, and chilli, caramelizes beautifully, creating a perfect blend of sweet, savoury, and spicy flavours that will gently kiss every part of your taste buds.

Prep: 10 minutes, Cook: 10 mins Servings: 2

Equipment

Medium bowl or resealable bag
Small bowl or measuring cup
Medium frying pan
Spatula

Ingredients

Salmon
340 g (12 oz) salmon fillet, skinless

Marinade
80 ml (⅓ cup) light soy sauce
115 g (⅓ cup) honey
4 garlic cloves, minced
2 tsp fresh ginger, minced
½ tsp chilli flakes
1 tbsp olive oil

For Cooking
1 tbsp olive oil

How to make it

Marinate the Salmon
In a small bowl, whisk together the soy sauce, honey, garlic, ginger, chilli flakes, and olive oil to make the marinade. Pour half of the marinade over the salmon in a resealable bag or medium bowl, saving the rest for later. Let it marinate in the fridge for at least 30 minutes.

Cook the Salmon
Heat 1 tbsp of olive oil in a medium frying pan over medium heat. Remove the salmon from the marinade and place it in the pan. Cook for 2-3 minutes on one side until golden, then flip and cook for another 1-2 minutes until done to your liking.

Make the Glaze
Remove the salmon and set it aside. Pour the reserved marinade into the pan, bringing it to a simmer. Let it reduce until it thickens into a sticky glaze (2-3 minutes).

Serve
Plate the salmon and drizzle the glaze over the top. Pair it with steamed broccoli, roasted veggies, or even some rice if you've got the setup.

Easy Chicken Katsu Curry

Ikuzo! Bring on the mighty Katsu curry but let's make this easy to do in your van without any compromise on flavour.

Prep: 15 minutes, Cook: 30 mins Servings: 2

Equipment

Stovetop
Manual blender (for the sauce)
Large frying pan
Medium saucepan
Knife and cutting board
Mixing bowls

Ingredients

Katsu Sauce
2 tbsp vegetable oil
6 garlic cloves, chopped
1 large onion, chopped
2 tsp honey
1 tbsp curry powder
3 tbsp plain flour
2 tbsp dark soy sauce
1 large carrot, chopped
700 ml chicken stock

Chicken
2 medium chicken breasts, trimmed and flattened to 1 inch thick
2 tbsp all-purpose flour
1 egg, whisked
1/2 cup panko breadcrumbs
4 tbsp vegetable oil (for shallow frying)

How to make it

For the Sauce
Heat 2 tbsp vegetable oil in a saucepan over a medium heat. Add the onion and cook until softened (about 8 minutes), stirring occasionally. Toss in the garlic and cook for 1-2 minutes.

Stir in the chopped carrot and let everything sauté for another 3 minutes.

Sprinkle in the curry powder, mixing well to coat the veggies. Cook for 2 minutes to toast the spices.
Gradually add the flour, stirring continuously until it forms a paste.

Slowly pour in the chicken stock, a little at a time, whisking to avoid lumps. Bring to a gentle simmer and cook for 5 minutes, allowing the flavors to meld.

Carefully transfer the mixture to your manual blender pot. Let it cool slightly (until there's no steam rising). Blend manually with 10-15 pulls until smooth–feel that arm workout!

Return the smooth sauce to the saucepan and bring back to a gentle simmer. Cook for 10-15 minutes, stirring occasionally. Season with soy sauce and honey, adjusting to taste. If it thickens too much, add a splash of water.

For the Chicken
Lightly season the chicken with salt.
Coat each breast in flour, then dip into the whisked egg, and finally press in the panko breadcrumbs to coat evenly.

Heat 4 tbsp of vegetable oil in a frying pan over medium heat. Shallow fry the chicken for 4-5 minutes per side, or until golden brown and cooked through. Transfer to a plate lined with paper towels to drain excess oil.

Slice the chicken and serve with the Katsu sauce and rice.

Korean Style Rolled Omelette

Gyeran Mari, or Korean rolled omelette, is the perfect quick bite for life on the road. It's savoury, packed with flavour, and surprisingly easy to whip up on a portable stove. Plus, it's a great way to use up those veggie odds and ends in your fridge.

Prep: 5 minutes, Cook: 8 mins Servings: 2

Equipment

Mixing bowl
Non-stick pan (about 20cm diameter)
Spatula
Fork or whisk

Ingredients

3 large eggs
2 tbsp milk
1 small spring onion, finely chopped
1 small carrot, finely diced (about 30g)
1 tbsp red bell pepper, finely diced
½ tsp soy sauce
½ tsp sesame oil
A pinch of salt
A touch of neutral oil (for frying)

No carrots? No problem. Swap in whatever veggies you've got on hand.
Make it extra fancy with a sprinkle of sesame seeds or a side of soy sauce for dipping.

How to make it

Prep the Mix
In a mixing bowl, whisk the eggs, milk, soy sauce, sesame oil, and salt until well combined. Toss in the chopped spring onion, carrot, and red bell pepper. Stir to evenly distribute the veggies.

Heat Things Up
Heat a small non-stick pan over low to medium heat and lightly grease it with a dab of neutral oil.

Cook the Layers
Pour a thin layer of the egg mixture into the pan–just enough to cover the bottom. Let it cook gently until the surface is almost set but still slightly wet.

Start Rolling
Using a spatula (or 2 spoons work well), lift one edge of the egg sheet and roll it towards the centre. Once rolled, push the omelette to one side of the pan.

Keep Rolling
Pour more egg mixture into the empty side of the pan, letting it connect to the roll. When this layer is mostly set, roll the omelette back over it. Repeat until all the egg mixture is used up.

Perfect and Serve
Remove the rolled omelette from the pan and let it rest for a minute before slicing it into bite-sized pieces.

Enjoy hot or at room temperature.

Butter Chicken

Butter chicken, or "murgh makhani," is a rich, creamy, and flavourful dish that's a staple of Indian cuisine. This version is vanlife-friendly, using simple ingredients to recreate a comforting restaurant favorite from your van stovetop.

Prep: 10 minutes, Cook: 20 mins Servings: 2

Equipment

Medium frying pan
Manual Blender
Wooden spoon

Ingredients

For the Chicken
250g chicken breast, diced
2 tbsp yoghurt
1/2 tsp garam masala
1/2 tsp turmeric
1/2 tsp chilli powder
1/2 tsp salt
1 tsp lemon juice
1 tbsp oil (for cooking)

For the Sauce
1 tbsp butter
1/2 small onion, finely chopped
2 cloves garlic, minced
1/2 inch ginger, grated
1/2 tsp cumin
1/2 tsp ground coriander
1/2 tsp garam masala
1/2 tsp chilli powder
1/2 cup chopped tomatoes
1/2 cup coconut milk or cream
1/2 tsp sugar
Handful of chopped cashew nuts
Handful of fresh coriander, chopped
Salt, to taste

How to make it

Marinate the Chicken
In a bowl, mix the chicken with yoghurt, garam masala, turmeric, chilli powder, salt, and lemon juice. Let it sit for at least 15 minutes (or longer if you've got the patience).

Cook the Chicken
Heat 1 tbsp oil in your pan over medium heat. Add the marinated chicken and cook for about 5-7 minutes until golden and cooked through. Remove and set aside.

Make the Sauce
In the same pan, melt the butter and sauté the onions until soft and golden. Add the garlic and ginger, cooking for another minute.

Stir in the cumin, coriander, garam masala, and paprika. Let them toast for 30 seconds to wake up the flavours. Pour in the chopped tomatoes, stirring well. Let it simmer for 5 minutes until it thickens slightly.

Add the coconut milk (or cream) and a pinch of sugar, if using. Stir everything together and let it bubble away for another 3-4 minutes.

Bring It All Together
Add the cooked chicken back into the sauce. Let it simmer for another 5 minutes so the flavours can mingle. Taste and adjust salt if needed.

Garnish
Before serving add a handful of fresh coriander and stir into the curry. Finally sprinkle over some chopped cashew nuts for that extra bite.

Indian Vegetable Chow Mein

This is a popular street food on the streets of India and is also popular in the Vanlife Eats van! It's nutritious, delicious, and super easy to make.

Prep: 10 minutes, Cook: 10 mins Servings: 2

Equipment

Large pan or wok
Mixing spoon
Manual Blender

Ingredients

2 small nests of medium-fine egg noodles, cooked as per the packet
½ tbsp dark soy sauce
1 tbsp sunflower oil
½ small red onion, thinly sliced
1 spring onion, finely chopped (white and green parts separated)
1 celery stick, finely chopped
½ green pepper, finely chopped
½ carrot, finely chopped
½-1 inch fresh ginger, finely chopped
2 garlic cloves, minced
1 small green chilli, finely chopped
½ tsp chilli sauce
½ tsp rice vinegar
Salt and Pepper to taste

How to make it

Cook the Aromatics
Heat the oil in a pan over medium heat. Throw in the ginger, garlic, and chilli, stirring for about a minute until they smell absolutely amazing.

Stir-Fry the Veg
Add the red onion, celery, carrot, green pepper, and the white bits of the spring onion. Stir-fry for around 5 minutes until they start to soften but still have a little crunch–no one likes soggy veg!

Adjust the Flavours
Sprinkle in the salt, black pepper, soy sauce, vinegar, and chilli sauce. Give it all a good mix so the veggies get properly coated in all the tasty goodness.

Toss in the Noodles
Add your cooked noodles, tossing everything together until they're warmed through and covered in all that flavour.

Garnish & Serve
Sprinkle the green parts of the spring onion on top, and boom–you're done!

Dig in straight from the pan or pile onto plates with an extra splash of chilli sauce.

Indonesian Fried Rice
Nasi Goreng

Nasi Goreng is Indonesia's answer to fried rice, packed with deep, caramelised flavours. This is a classic way to turn leftover rice into something outrageously good. Traditionally, it's topped with a crispy fried egg, cucumber, and fresh tomato.

Prep: 5 minutes, Cook: 10 mins Servings: 2

Equipment

Large pan or wok
Manual blender
Spatula
Small bowl

Ingredients

Rice & Sauce
2 cups cooked white rice (cold, day-old rice works best but packet rice will do!)
1 small onion, diced
2 cloves garlic, finely chopped
1 tsp red chilli, finely chopped (or to taste)
1 tbsp oil
3 tbsp light soy sauce
3 tbsp brown sugar
2 tsp shrimp paste (optional, but worth it!)

Protein
150g chicken breast, thinly sliced (or swap for shrimp, tofu, beef, or pork)
1 tbsp oil

Toppings & Sides
2 eggs, fried to perfection (runny yolk = extra delicious)
1 spring onion, sliced
Tomato & cucumber, cut into wedges

How to make it

Make a Sweet Soy Sauce
In a small bowl mix together the light soy sauce and the brown sugar and place to one side.

Heat 1 tbsp of oil in your pan over medium-high heat. Add the chicken and cook for a couple of minutes until it turns mostly white. Drizzle in 1 tbsp of the sweet soy sauce and let it cook for another minute until slightly caramelised. Remove and set aside.

In the same pan, add the remaining oil. Toss in the garlic and chilli, stir for 10 seconds, then add the onion. Cook for about a minute until the onion softens.

Add the cooked rice, the remaining sweet soy sauce, and shrimp paste (if using). Stir continuously for 2-3 minutes until everything is well-coated and slightly caramelised.

Return the chicken to the pan, mix everything together, and cook for another minute.

Serve with a fried egg on top, a sprinkle of spring onions, and any of the optional garnishes. A squeeze of lime? Yes, please.

Pork Belly Bao Buns

Think of a bacon and egg sandwich but Asian style! Fluffy buns, crispy pork, and a runny egg–what's not to love?

Prep: 5 minutes, Cook: 10 mins Servings: 2

Equipment

Frying pan
Spatula
Knife
Chopping board

Ingredients

2 bao buns
200g pork belly, sliced
2 eggs
2 spring onions, finely sliced
Chilli sauce or Korean BBQ sauce

How to make it

Toast the Buns
Heat a dry pan over medium heat and lightly toast the bao buns until warm and slightly golden. Watch them closely–nobody likes a burnt bun.

Cook the Pork
In the same pan, fry the pork belly slices over medium-high heat until crispy and golden. Flip occasionally to get that perfect caramelisation.

Fry the Eggs
When the pork is nearly done, push it to the side of the pan and crack in the eggs. Cook sunny-side up until the whites are set but the yolks are still runny.

Assemble
Place the crispy pork belly inside the bao buns, drizzle with your choice of chilli sauce or Korean BBQ sauce, and carefully slide a fried egg on top.

Final Touches
Sprinkle over the sliced spring onions, pop the lid on, and get stuck in!

Pork Belly Bao Buns with Caramelised Apple

Sweet, savoury, and packed with flavour, this twist on the classic bao bun swaps the egg for caramelised apple slices. The pork belly stays crispy, the bao buns stay fluffy, and the apples add just the right amount of sweetness to balance the richness.

Prep: 5 minutes, Cook: 10 mins Servings: 2

Equipment

Frying pan
Spatula
Knife
Chopping board

Ingredients

2 bao buns
200g pork belly, sliced
½ apple, thinly sliced (Braeburn or Pink Lady work well)
1 tsp honey or maple syrup
2 spring onions, finely sliced
Chilli sauce or Korean BBQ sauce

How to make it

Toast the Buns
Heat a dry pan over medium heat and lightly toast the bao buns until warm and slightly golden. Keep an eye on them–you want toasted, not charred.

Cook the Pork
In the same pan, fry the pork belly slices over medium-high heat until crispy and golden, flipping occasionally to ensure even browning.

Caramelise the Apples
Once the pork is nearly done, move it to one side of the pan. Add butter, then toss in the apple slices. Drizzle with honey (or maple syrup) and cook for 1-2 minutes until soft and slightly golden.

Assemble
Place the crispy pork belly inside the bao buns, drizzle with your choice of chilli sauce or Korean BBQ sauce, and top with the caramelised apple slices.

Final Touches
Scatter over the spring onions, pop the lid on, and take a big bite.

Malaysian Coconut Rice and Spicy Sambal

Nasi lemak is the ultimate comfort food in Malaysia, and when I make this, it never fails to excite my taste buds. The spice from the sambal is balanced by the creaminess of the coconut rice, and then the cucumber freshens you up. It really is fireworks in your mouth!

Prep: 10 minutes, Cook: 30 mins Servings: 2

Equipment

Saucepan with a lid
Small frying pan
Spatula
Bowl
Knife & chopping board

Ingredients

For the Coconut Rice
150g (¾ cup) jasmine rice, rinsed
200ml (¾ cup) coconut milk
100ml (⅓ cup) water
¼ tsp salt

For the Sambal (Spicy Sauce)
1 tbsp oil
1 small onion, finely chopped
1 garlic clove, minced
2 red chillies
½ tsp sugar
½ tsp salt
1 tsp tamarind paste (or a squeeze of lime juice)

For the Toppings
2 boiled eggs, halved
25g (¼ cup) peanuts, toasted
4 cucumber slices
Any protein you would like goes with this. I used pork belly in the photo.

How to make it

Cook the Coconut Rice
In a saucepan, combine the rinsed rice, coconut milk, water, and salt.

Bring to a simmer over low heat, cover, and let it cook for about 15 minutes. Until it looks like it is drying out.

Turn off the heat and let it steam for another 10 minutes before fluffing it with a fork.

Make the Sambal
Heat the oil in a small pan over medium heat.

Sauté the onion and garlic until soft and fragrant, about 2 minutes.

Toss in the chopped chillies and cook for another 2 minutes.

Stir in the sugar, salt, and tamarind paste (or lime juice). Cook for 1 more minute, then remove from heat.

Assemble the Nasi Lemak
Plate up the coconut rice in the centre.

Arrange the boiled eggs, toasted peanuts, cucumber slices, and your chosen protein around it.

Spoon the sambal over the rice or on the side (if you're playing it safe with spice).

optional: Serve with your protein of choice

Lamb Curry Pie

Who says pie needs an oven? Thanks to Omnia, this hearty lamb and potato curry pie is proof that you can get a golden, flaky crust straight from your van's stovetop. Tender lamb, spiced potatoes, and a rich, fragrant curry sauce, all wrapped up in a crispy shortcrust pastry.

Prep: 15 minutes, Cook: 45 mins Servings: 2 - 4

Equipment

Omnia stovetop oven (no liner)
Manual blender (or a knife and determination)
Frying pan
Mixing bowl
Pastry brush
Knife & chopping board

Ingredients

300g lamb, cut into small pieces and dusted with flour
1 medium potato, diced
1 red onion, roughly chopped
2 garlic cloves, peeled
Thumb-sized piece of fresh ginger, peeled
200g chopped tinned tomatoes
½ tsp ground cumin
½ tsp turmeric
½ tsp ground coriander
¼ tsp chilli powder (adjust to taste)
1 tsp garam masala
1 lamb stock cube, dissolved in 150ml hot water
1 tbsp rapeseed oil
1 sheet pre-made shortcrust pastry
1 egg, beaten (for egg wash)
Fresh coriander
Butter (for greasing)

How to make it

Heat the rapeseed oil in a frying pan over medium heat. Add the lamb pieces and fry until browned. Scoop them out and set aside.

Blend the onion, garlic, and ginger into a rough paste.

In the same pan, add the cumin, turmeric, coriander, and chilli powder. Toast them for about 30 seconds and then add the paste.

Stir in the chopped tomatoes, then add the diced potatoes and garam masala.

Return the lamb to the pan, pour in the lamb stock, and let everything simmer for about 20 minutes until the potatoes are tender and the sauce thickens. Stir in the fresh coriander. It shouldn't be too wet–this is pie!

Butter the base of the Omnia oven. Roll out the shortcrust pastry and press it into the Omnia base, leaving some extra around the edges to seal the top later.

Spoon the slightly cooled filling into the pastry-lined Omnia.
Roll out the remaining pastry and cut a lid to fit the top. Get creative–make it fancy with strips or just go classic with a full lid.

Seal the edges, cut a few steam vents, and brush with egg wash.

Place the Omnia over medium-low heat and cook for about 45 minutes, until the pastry is golden and crisp.

Carefully flip the pie out onto a plate (or just dig in straight from the Omnia–zero judgment here).

Vegetable Manchurian

A delightful Indo-Chinese dish, Vegetable Manchurian is a popular street food in India, blending the richness of vegetables with savoury soy-based flavors. Typically served with fried rice or noodles, this versatile recipe is a favorite in the Mumbai and Kolkata street food scenes.

Prep: 5 minutes, Cook: 25 mins Servings: 24 Balls

Equipment

Deep Saucepan
Manual blender
Wooden spoon
Slotted spoon
Knife & chopping board

Ingredients

For the Vegetable Balls
½ small cabbage, grated
1 carrot, grated
100 g (3½ oz) fine green beans, finely chopped
2 green chillies, finely chopped
100 g (3½ oz) plain flour
1 tsp salt
2 tbsp cornflour

For the Sauce
1 tbsp sunflower oil
1 green chilli, finely chopped
2 garlic cloves, finely chopped
2.5 cm (1 inch) piece of fresh ginger, finely chopped
2 celery sticks, finely chopped
1 tbsp soy sauce
1 tsp rice vinegar
¼ tsp salt
700 ml (1¼ pints) vegetable stock
2 tbsp cornflour
1 tbsp water

How to make it

To Make the Vegetable Balls
Combine all the ingredients for the vegetable balls in a large bowl. Mix thoroughly until the mixture starts to stick together. Shape into lime-sized balls–this recipe should make about 24 balls.

Heat sunflower oil in a deep, heavy saucepan to 180°C (350°F). Line a plate with kitchen paper.

Fry the vegetable balls in batches, turning occasionally, for 2 minutes on each side or until golden brown. Transfer the fried balls to the kitchen paper to drain off excess oil.

To Prepare the Sauce
Heat 1 tablespoon of sunflower oil in a wide saucepan over medium heat. Add the chili, garlic, ginger, and celery, cooking for 5 minutes until the celery softens.
Stir in the soy sauce, vinegar, salt, and vegetable stock. Bring to a boil.

In a small bowl, mix the cornflour with 1 tablespoon of water to form a smooth paste. Slowly stir this paste into the sauce. Cook over a high heat for 2 minutes, or until the sauce thickens slightly.

Final Assembly
Add the fried vegetable balls to the sauce and let them steep for about 5 minutes, ensuring they absorb the flavors.
Serve hot with rice or noodles, if desired.

Pav Bhaji

A flavorful street food classic from Mumbai, Pav Bhaji is a delicious blend of mashed vegetables and spices, served with buttery rolls. This simplified version is hearty, easy to make, and ideal for one-pan cooking.

Prep: 10 minutes, Cook: 25 mins Servings: 2

Equipment

Wide saucepan or skillet
Potato masher or fork

Ingredients

For the Bhaji

1 tbsp sunflower oil
1 tbsp salted butter, plus extra for serving
1/2 onion, finely chopped
1 tomato, finely chopped
1/2 small cauliflower, grated or finely chopped (about 200 g)
1/2 green pepper, finely chopped
300 ml (10 oz) water, divided
1 tsp salt, or to taste
1 tbsp Pav Bhaji Masala (or your favorite garam masala blend)
2 medium potatoes, boiled, peeled, and grated
Handful of fresh coriander, finely chopped

To Serve

2 soft bread rolls, split horizontally
1-2 tbsp butter for toasting
Lime wedges

How to make it

Cook the Vegetables

Heat the oil and butter in a wide saucepan over medium heat. Add the onion and cook for 5 minutes until softened. Stir in the tomato, cauliflower, green pepper, and 150 ml (5 oz) of the water. Bring to a boil, then cover with a lid and simmer for 15 minutes, stirring occasionally.

Season and Mash

Stir in the salt and Pav Bhaji Masala, cooking for 2 minutes. Add the grated potatoes and the remaining 150 ml (5 oz) water. Mash the mixture directly in the pan using a potato masher or fork, ensuring a chunky yet cohesive texture. Cook for another 5 minutes, stirring well.

Toast the Rolls

In a separate frying pan (or using the same pan once the Bhaji is done), melt the butter over medium heat. Toast the bread roll halves for 1 minute on each side until golden.

Serve

Garnish the Bhaji with fresh coriander and serve with the buttered rolls on the side. Squeeze lime juice over the Bhaji before enjoying.

Chicken Tikka Masala

Being the national dish of Britain, I needed to master this one! Not only that, but I love it! Being rich and deep in tomato and spices, it was immediately on my radar.

Prep: 10 minutes, Cook: 20 mins Servings: 2

Equipment

Large pan
Mixing bowl
Chopping board
Knife
Spoon/spatula

Ingredients

For the Chicken
250g chicken breast, diced
2 tbsp yoghurt
½ tsp cumin
½ tsp paprika
½ tsp turmeric
½ tsp salt
1 tsp lemon juice
1 tbsp oil (for cooking)

For the Sauce
1 tbsp butter
½ small onion, finely chopped
2 cloves garlic, minced
½ inch ginger, grated
½ tsp garam masala
½ tsp ground coriander
½ tsp chilli powder
½ cup chopped tomatoes
¼ cup cream
½ tsp sugar
Handful of fresh coriander, chopped
Salt, to taste

How to make it

Marinate the Chicken
In a bowl, mix the diced chicken with yoghurt, cumin, paprika, turmeric, salt, and lemon juice. Let it sit for at least 15 minutes–longer if you can.

Cook the Chicken
Heat 1 tbsp of oil in a pan over medium heat. Toss in the marinated chicken and cook for about 5-7 minutes until golden and fully cooked. Remove and set aside.

Make the Sauce
In the same pan, melt the butter and sauté the onions until soft and golden. Add the garlic and ginger, stirring for another minute.

Now, toss in the garam masala, ground coriander, and chilli powder–give them 30 seconds to wake up and start smelling incredible.

Pour in the chopped tomatoes, stirring well. Let them simmer for 5 minutes until they thicken slightly.

Add the cream and a pinch of sugar. Stir everything together and let it bubble away for another 3-4 minutes.

Bring It All Together
Slide the cooked chicken back into the pan, stirring it through the sauce. Let it simmer for another 5 minutes so all those flavours come together. Taste and adjust the salt if needed.

Finishing Touches
Before serving, stir in a handful of fresh coriander and a splosh of cream. That's it–you've just made a killer Tikka Masala in your tiny kitchen.

Serve with rice or naan bread.

Potato Fritter Sandwich

Vada Pav, a quintessential Mumbai street food, is perfect for breakfast, lunch, or dinner. This spicy, flavour-packed potato fritter sandwich is easy to prepare in your tiny kitchen with minimal equipment.

Prep: 15 minutes, Cook: 35 mins Servings: 2

Equipment

Frying pan
Mixing bowls
Slotted spoon

Ingredients

For the Vada
1/2 tbsp sunflower oil
1/2 tsp black mustard seeds
4 curry leaves
1 small green chilli, finely chopped
1 garlic clove, finely chopped
1/2-inch piece of fresh ginger, peeled and finely chopped
1/2 tsp salt
1/4 tsp ground turmeric
2 medium potatoes, boiled, peeled, and mashed

For the Batter
50g (1/2 cup) gram (chickpea) flour
1/4 tsp salt
1/4 tsp ground turmeric
Water (as needed, to make a thick batter)

To Serve
4 small bread rolls (such as dinner rolls or burger buns), split horizontally
Coriander and Spinach Chutney
Chilli and Garlic Chutney
Sea salt flakes, for garnish (optional)

How to make it

Peel, boil and mash your potato.
You can do this earlier in the day, or use leftovers.

Prepare the Spiced Potato Mixture
Heat the sunflower oil in a frying pan over medium heat. Add the mustard seeds, and when they start popping, add the curry leaves, green chilli, garlic, ginger, salt, and turmeric. Sauté for 1-2 minutes, then mix in the mashed potatoes. Cook for another 2 minutes, stirring until combined. Set aside to cool.

Shape the Vadas
Divide the spiced potato mixture into 4 equal portions and shape each into a ball or patty.

Make the Batter
In a mixing bowl, combine the gram flour, salt, and turmeric. Gradually whisk in enough water to form a smooth, thick batter.

Fry the Vadas
Heat a thin layer of sunflower oil in a frying pan. Dip each potato ball into the batter, ensuring it's fully coated, and fry in the oil for 2-3 minutes per side, until golden brown and crisp. Remove with a slotted spoon and drain on paper towels.

Assemble the Vada Pav
Spread Coriander and Spinach Chutney on one half of each bread roll and Chilli and Garlic Chutney on the other half. Place a hot vada in the middle, sprinkle with sea salt flakes (if using), and close the roll.

Serve
Enjoy your Vada Pav fresh and hot as a hearty snack or meal on the go!

Hoisin Beef Lettuce Wraps

These Hoisin Beef Lettuce Wraps combine fresh, crisp textures with savoury, tangy beef for a light yet satisfying vanlife meal. The no-bread approach makes them portable, mess-free, and perfect for sharing.

Prep: 15 minutes, Cook: 10 mins Servings: 2

Equipment

Medium saucepan
Nonstick frying pan
Mixing bowls

Ingredients

100g (3.5 oz) rice noodles
1/2 yellow bell pepper, thinly sliced
1 small carrot, julienned
1/4 daikon radish, julienned
60ml (1/4 cup) rice wine vinegar
250g (9 oz) beef sirloin, thinly sliced
60ml (1/4 cup) hoisin sauce
Juice of 1/2 lemon
2 cloves garlic, finely chopped
1/4 tsp red chilli, finely chopped (optional)
Kosher salt, to taste
Large iceberg lettuce leaves, for wrapping
2 tbsp fresh cilantro, chopped
1 tbsp fresh basil, chopped

How to make it

Prepare the Noodles and Vegetables
Cook the rice noodles in salted water according to package instructions, about 5-7 minutes. Drain and set aside at room temperature.
Slice the bell pepper and julienne the carrot and radish. Add the vegetables to a bowl. Toss with the rice wine vinegar for a quick pickling and set aside.

Marinate and Cook the Beef
In a small bowl, mix the hoisin sauce, half the lemon juice, and garlic. Add the beef slices, ensuring they're evenly coated. Heat a nonstick pan over medium-high heat and cook the marinated beef for 5-6 minutes, turning occasionally, until browned and cooked to your preference. Remove from heat.

Deglaze the Pan
Add the remaining hoisin sauce and a splash of water to the pan to loosen the flavourful bits. Let it cook for 1-2 minutes, stirring to combine. Toss the beef back in to coat it with the sauce.

Assemble the Wraps
Lay out sturdy iceberg lettuce leaves. Layer each with a portion of beef, pickled vegetables, and rice noodles. Garnish with cilantro, basil, and a squeeze of fresh lemon juice.

Serve
Wrap the ingredients tightly in the lettuce leaves for easy handling and enjoy immediately.

Pakistani Biryani

Biryani is one of those dishes that makes you forget you're cooking in a tiny van kitchen. This version keeps all the bold, aromatic flavours of a proper Pakistani biryani, but we're making it van-friendly–one pan, stovetop only, and no stress.

Prep: 35 minutes, Cook: 25 mins Servings: 2

Equipment

Large deep pan with a lid
Small pot
Cutting board
Knife
Spatula or spoon

Ingredients

For the Rice
1 cup basmati rice, rinsed and soaked for 30 minutes
2 cups water
½ tsp salt
2 green cardamom pods
1 small cinnamon stick
2 cloves
For the Saffron Milk
2 tbsp warm milk
A pinch of saffron strands
For the Masala
1 small onion, thinly sliced
1 small tomato, chopped
200g chicken (thighs or breast), cut into bite-sized pieces
2 tbsp plain yoghurt
½ tsp turmeric
½ tsp red chilli powder
½ tsp garam masala
½ tsp ground cumin
½ tsp ground coriander
1 small potato, peeled and diced (optional but highly recommended)
1 tsp ginger-garlic paste
2 tbsp oil or ghee
Salt, to taste
For Garnish
Fresh coriander, chopped
Fried onions (if you've got them)
A squeeze of lemon

How to make it

Infuse the Saffron Milk
In a small bowl, mix the saffron strands with warm milk and set aside to develop its deep golden colour.

Cook the Rice
Bring 2 cups of water to a boil in a small pot. Add salt, cardamom, cinnamon, and cloves. Stir in the soaked rice and cook until it's about 80% done–soft but still holding its shape. Drain and set aside.

Prepare the Masala
Heat oil or ghee in your deep pan over medium heat. Add sliced onions and fry until golden brown. Stir in the ginger-garlic paste and cook for 30 seconds.

Add the Spices
Toss in the chopped tomatoes, turmeric, chilli powder, cumin, coriander, and salt. Let this cook until the tomatoes break down into a thick masala base.

Cook the Chicken & Potatoes
Add the chicken pieces, coating them well in the masala. Stir in the yoghurt and let it simmer for 10 minutes. If using potatoes, add them now and cook until tender.

Layering the Biryani
Once the chicken is fully cooked, lower the heat. Spread the cooked rice over the masala in an even layer without stirring. Drizzle the saffron milk over the top for that signature colour and fragrance.

Steam it Up
Cover the pan with a lid (or foil) and let it steam on low heat for 10 minutes to let the flavours meld.

Final Touches
Turn off the heat and let the biryani sit for 5 minutes before fluffing it up with a fork. Garnish with fresh coriander, fried onions, and a squeeze of lemon.

Serve hot with raita or a simple yoghurt dip.

Easy Chicken Pad Thai

This one's for those nights when you want big flavour with minimal faff. Pad Thai is a street food classic, but we're making it van-friendly with no comprimise on flavour!

Prep: 30 minutes, Cook: 15 mins Servings: 2

Equipment

Large frying pan or wok
Small saucepan
Knife & chopping board
Tongs or spatula

Ingredients

100g (3.5 oz) thin dried rice noodles
50g (1.7 oz) firm tofu, diced
2 chicken breasts, diced
1 tbsp vegetable oil
1 small shallot, sliced
2 eggs, lightly whisked
1/2 cup spring onions, finely sliced
1/2 cup bean shoots, plus extra to serve
1 tbsp crushed peanuts
Lime wedges, to serve
Chilli powder, to serve
Spring onion stems, to serve

For the Sauce
50g (1.7 oz) fish sauce
50g (1.7 oz) tamarind concentrate
60g (2 oz) dark brown sugar
¼ tsp dark soy sauce

How to make it

Get the prep done
Soak the rice noodles in room temperature water for about 30 minutes or until softened but still firm. Once softened, boil them for 3-4 minutes until just tender. Drain and keep them handy.

Make the sauce
In a small saucepan over medium-high heat, combine the fish sauce, tamarind concentrate, brown sugar, and dark soy sauce. Stir until the sugar dissolves, then remove from heat and set aside.

Cook it up
Heat oil in your frying pan over high heat. Toss in the shallot and fry for about 30 seconds. Add the chicken pieces and cook until nearly done, then throw in the tofu. Stir-fry for another 30 seconds.

Add Egg
Push everything to one side of the pan, then pour the eggs into the empty space. Let them set slightly before breaking them up and mixing them through the rest of the ingredients.

Bring it all together
Add the noodles and pour over the sauce. Stir-fry until everything is well coated, then toss through the spring onions and bean shoots.

Serve it up
Dish up onto plates, sprinkle over the crushed peanuts, and serve with lime wedges, extra bean shoots, a pinch of chilli powder, and a few spring onion stems for crunch.

RidgeMonkey

Tibetan Momos

Little dumplings packed with flavour! These Tibetan momos are fun to make, easy to customise, and ridiculously satisfying–whether you go for the veggie version or the juicy pork filling. Plus, they're the perfect excuse to dunk something in chilli sauce.

Prep: 20 minutes, Cook: 10 mins Servings: 2

Equipment

Bowl (for mixing dough)
Manual blender (or just some determined chopping)
Rolling pin (or a bottle if you're improvising)
Knife & cutting board
Pan with lid (for steaming)

Ingredients

Dough
1 cup (120g) plain flour
1/4 cup (60ml) water (adjust as needed)

Veggie Filling
1/2 cup (40g) cabbage, finely chopped
1/2 small onion, finely chopped
1 small carrot, grated
1 clove garlic, minced
1cm fresh ginger, minced

Pork Filling (for the meaty option)
100g pork mince
1/2 small onion, finely chopped
1/2 tsp salt

For Serving
Pickled red onion (soaked in apple cider vinegar)
Chilli sauce (essential, obviously)
Fresh coriander, for garnish

How to make it

Make the Pickled Red Onion
Finely slice half an onion and leave it to soak in some apple cider vinegar. Set to one side and wait for the colour change.

Make the Dough
In a bowl, mix the flour and water until a dough forms. Knead it for a few minutes until it's smooth and elastic–think playdough, but edible. Cover and let it rest while you prep the filling.

Prep the Filling
If making the veggie version, blend or finely chop the cabbage, onion, ginger, carrot, and garlic.

For the pork filling, season the pork, blend or finely chop the onion, then mix it with the pork mince.

Whatever option, just make sure everything is well combined.

Shape the Momos
Roll out the dough and cut it into small discs, about the size of your palm. Place a spoonful of filling in the centre of each disc, then pinch the edges together to seal. You can pleat them if you're feeling fancy, or just squish them shut.

Cook the Momos
Heat a little oil in your pan over medium heat. Place the momos in and let them sizzle for a minute to get a golden bottom. Then, add a splash of water and pop the lid on to steam them for about 8 minutes, until the dough is cooked through.

Serve It Up
Plate up your momos with pickled red onion, a generous drizzle of chilli sauce, and a handful of fresh coriander.

Indian Spiced Meatball Curry

Juicy, flavour-packed meatballs simmered in a rich, aromatic sauce make this dish a proper comfort meal. Best enjoyed with fluffy rice, warm flatbreads, or even straight from the pan!

Prep: 15 minutes, Cook: 25 mins Servings: 2

Equipment

Mixing bowl
Large frying pan with a lid
Chopping board & knife
Wooden spoon
Grater

Ingredients

For the Meatballs
200g minced lamb (or beef)
1 tbsp gram flour (or plain flour)
½ tsp cumin powder
½ tsp garam masala
½ tsp salt
1 garlic clove, minced
½ tsp grated ginger
½ green chilli, finely chopped
Small handful of coriander, chopped

For the Curry Sauce
1 small onion, finely chopped
1 tbsp oil (vegetable or coconut)
2 garlic cloves, minced
½ tsp ginger, grated
½ tsp ground turmeric
1 tsp ground coriander
½ tsp chilli powder
1 tsp cumin seeds
1 large tomato, grated
200ml coconut milk
½ tsp salt
Juice of ½ a lime
Fresh coriander for garnish

How to make it

Make the Meatballs
In a bowl, mix the minced lamb (or beef) with gram flour, cumin, garam masala, salt, minced garlic, ginger, and chopped green chilli. Use your hands to combine everything until the mixture is just sticking together. Form into small, bite-sized meatballs.

Heat a little oil in your pan over medium heat. Add the meatballs and cook, turning occasionally, until they're browned all over but not fully cooked through. Remove and set aside.

In the same pan, add more oil if needed and toss in the cumin seeds. Let them sizzle for a few seconds before adding the chopped onion. Sauté until soft and golden, then stir in the garlic and ginger. Cook for another minute until fragrant.

Sprinkle in the turmeric, coriander, chilli powder, and salt. Stir well, then add the grated tomato. Cook for a few minutes until it thickens slightly. Pour in the coconut milk and stir to combine.

Return the meatballs to the pan, nestling them into the sauce. Cover with a lid and let them simmer for about 10 minutes, stirring occasionally, until cooked through. If the sauce gets too thick, add a splash of water.

Squeeze over the lime juice and scatter fresh coriander on top. Serve hot with rice or naan..or both!

Cheese and Onion Bhaji Burgers

Crispy, golden bhaji patties stuffed with gooey cheddar, packed into a soft bun–it's a game-changer. These beauties bring together the crunchy goodness of an onion bhaji with the melty magic of cheese, all in burger form.

Prep: 10 minutes, Cook: 15 mins Servings: 2

Equipment

Mixing bowl
Grater
Frying pan
Spatula

Ingredients

1 large onion, grated
50g (½ cup) gram flour (chickpea flour)
½ tsp ground cumin
½ tsp ground coriander
¼ tsp turmeric
¼ tsp chilli powder (optional, but recommended)
A pinch of salt
50g (½ cup) cheddar cheese, grated
2 tbsp water
Oil, for frying
2 burger buns
Handful of fresh coriander, chopped (optional, but makes you look fancy)
Lettuce leaves
Apple chutney

How to make it

In a bowl, mix the grated onion with gram flour, cumin, coriander, turmeric, chilli powder, and salt. Stir in the water to form a thick batter. It should hold together but not be too runny.

Fold the grated cheddar into the batter. If it looks like a questionable mess, you're on the right track.

Heat a little oil in a frying pan over medium heat. Scoop out a handful of the mixture and flatten it into a rough patty shape. Fry for about 3-4 minutes per side until golden and crisp.

Pop the crispy bhaji patties into burger buns, throw in some fresh coriander, lettuce, and some apple chutney.

Words can't explain any further!

Spinach and Feta Borek

Warm, flaky, and oh-so-satisfying–this Turkish-inspired borek is your ticket to a fuss-free vanlife brunch. With minimal ingredients and a little stovetop magic, you'll have a golden, crispy delight ready to impress.

Prep: 15 minutes, Cook: 60 mins Servings: 2

Equipment

Omnia stovetop oven (no silicone liner)
Small frying pan
Mixing bowl
Pastry brush

Ingredients

2 cups (200g) fresh spinach, chopped
1/2 cup (100g) feta cheese, crumbled
2 large sheets of filo pastry
2 tbsp olive oil (plus extra for spraying)
1 egg, lightly beaten
1/4 tsp black pepper
1/4 tsp red pepper flakes (optional, for a spicy kick)

How to make it

Sauté the Spinach
Heat 1 tablespoon of olive oil in a small frying pan. Add the chopped spinach and cook over medium heat until wilted (2-3 minutes). Remove from heat and let it cool slightly. Squeeze out as much excess liquid as you can.

Prepare the Filling
In a mixing bowl, combine the cooked spinach, crumbled feta cheese, black pepper, and red pepper flakes (if using). Stir until evenly mixed.

Layer the Filo Pastry
Lay out one sheet of filo pastry on your campervan worktop (or a clean, flat surface). Spray lightly with olive oil, then layer a second sheet on top, ensuring you spray oil between the layers to prevent sticking.

Add the Filling
At the top edge of the filo, spread a line of the spinach-feta mixture about 1 inch wide. Roll the pastry over the filling to form a thin log. Repeat the process with another line of filling until you've used it all and formed a long, multi-layered roll.

Shape and Place in the Omnia
Spray the base of your Omnia oven generously with olive oil (skip the silicone liner for this recipe). Carefully coil the pastry roll into the circular base, joining the ends to form a ring.

Brush and Bake
Brush the top of the pastry with beaten egg for that golden finish. Place the Omnia on the stovetop and cook over low heat for 1 hour. Keep the heat low to ensure even cooking without burning the bottom.

Cool and Serve
Remove the borek carefully from the Omnia (it's delicate). Let it cool slightly before slicing and serving warm.

AFRICA

In Nigeria, there's a street food so powerful, it's basically natural Viagra!

It's called Suya—spicy, flame-grilled meat skewers coated in a top-secret peanut spice blend. But here's the kicker: Nigerian men swear it boosts their "performance" in ways even science can't explain.

Msemen

Crispy on the outside, soft and layered on the inside–Msemen is Morocco's answer to a pancake, but with way more attitude. These square-shaped flatbreads are flaky, golden, and perfect for scooping up stews or drizzling with honey. No oven, no fuss–just simple ingredients and a hot pan.

Prep: 45 minutes, Cook: 20 mins Servings: 6

Equipment

Skillet or frying pan
Mixing bowl
Measuring cups
Rolling pin (or just your hands)

Ingredients

For the Dough
1 cup plain flour
¾ cup fine semolina flour
¼ tsp dry active yeast
½ tsp salt
1 tsp sugar
1 ¼ cups warm water (add gradually)
Extra flour for kneading

For Folding & Cooking
4 tbsp sunflower oil (for the pan & rolling surface)
4 tbsp extra semolina flour (for layering)
¼ tsp baking powder
2 tbsp butter (optional, for extra richness)

How to make it

Make the Dough
In a bowl, mix the plain flour, semolina flour, salt, sugar, and yeast.
Slowly add warm water, mixing with a spoon until a dough forms.
Knead on a lightly floured surface for about 5 minutes until soft and springy.

Divide the dough into 6 balls and place them on a lightly oiled surface.
Cover with a damp tea towel and let them rest for 30 minutes.
Meanwhile, mix the baking powder with the extra semolina flour for later –this helps create flaky layers.

Shape & Fold
Take one dough ball at a time and roll (or press) it into a thin rectangle on a lightly oiled surface.
Dot a few small spots of butter over the surface and sprinkle a little semolina mix.
Fold the top and bottom edges to the middle, then overlap them like an envelope.
Sprinkle a bit more semolina mix, then fold in the sides to form a small square parcel.
Repeat with all dough balls, covering them to prevent drying out.

Cook the Msemen
Heat a pan over medium heat with a splash of oil.
Take one parcel at a time and press it out into a larger square.
Sprinkle with a little more semolina mix and place in the hot pan.
Cook for about 2 minutes per side, flipping once golden and puffed up.
Flip again for an extra minute on each side for extra crispiness.

Serve It Up
Msemen is traditionally served with honey and butter, but it's just as good with jam, cheese, or even a savoury stew.

Egyptian Filo Meat Pie

Get ready to tackle this Egyptian-inspired savoury delight with nothing but your trusty Omnia stovetop oven. It's all about crispy layers of Filo, a spiced beef filling, and some vanlife ingenuity!

Prep: 10 minutes, Cook: 45 mins Servings: 2-4

Equipment

Omnia stovetop oven (no silicone liner needed)
Mixing bowl
Large skillet
Silicone pastry brush (optional)
Sharp knife

Ingredients

For the beef filling
1 tbsp olive oil
1 small onion, finely chopped
680g (1.5 lbs) lean ground beef
1 tsp ground allspice
½ tsp ground black pepper (or to taste)
1 tsp salt (I went with pink salt!)
¼ tsp ground cinnamon
¼ tsp ground ginger
1 tbsp tomato paste

For the filo layers
200g (approx. 8 sheets) filo dough, thawed
Light olive oil spray (or ½ cup light olive oil for brushing)
¼ cup melted butter or ghee
1 large egg
1 cup milk
Salt and pepper to taste

How to make it

Prepare the filling
Heat olive oil in the base of your Omnia (no liner) over high heat. Add the onion and sauté for 2-3 minutes until softened. Toss in the ground beef and break it apart as it cooks. Stir in the allspice, black pepper, salt, cinnamon, ginger, and tomato paste. Cook until the beef is browned and no pink remains. Transfer the filling to a bowl and set aside.

Layer the filo in the Omnia
Wipe down the base of the Omnia and spray it lightly with olive oil. Lay a sheet of filo dough into the base, letting the edges drape over. Spray or brush it with olive oil and melted butter. Repeat with 3-4 more sheets, oiling between each layer.

Add the filling and top with filo
Spoon the cooked beef mixture into the filo-lined Omnia and spread evenly. Cover with the remaining filo sheets, layering and oiling as before. Tuck in or fold over any overhanging edges to seal the pie.

Make the milk-egg wash
In a small bowl, whisk together the egg, milk, salt, and pepper. Gently pour the mixture over the assembled pie and brush with a pastry brush.

Cook on the stovetop
Place the Omnia over medium-low heat on your stove. Cover with the lid and cook for about 35-45 minutes. The filo should turn golden and crispy. Careful not to burn the base.

Cool and serve
Let the pie cool for a few minutes before slicing it directly in the Omnia or VERY carefully removing it from the Omnia. Serve warm.

Vanlife Eats

Moroccan Lamb Koftas in a Spicy Tomato Sauce

Juicy, flavour-packed lamb koftas meet a rich, spiced tomato sauce - perfect for scooping up with warm pittas or fluffy couscous. This is one of those deceptively simple dishes that makes you feel like a pro chef!

Prep: 15 minutes, Cook: 25 mins Servings: 2

Equipment

Large frying pan or deep skillet (with a lid)
Sharp knife
Chopping board
Wooden spoon
Measuring cups & spoons

Ingredients

For the Koftas
250g lamb mince
½ tsp ground coriander
½ small red onion, finely chopped
½ tbsp fresh mint, chopped
Salt & pepper, to taste

For the Sauce
½ tbsp olive oil
1 garlic clove, finely chopped
1 x 400g can chopped tomatoes
1 tsp harissa (or more if you like it fiery)
½ tsp sugar
Salt & pepper, to taste

For Serving
100g Greek yogurt
Warm pittas or couscous

How to make it

Prep the Koftas
Get your hands in there - mix the lamb mince with the onion, coriander, mint, and a good pinch of salt and pepper. Shape the mixture into 4 small sausage-like shapes, roughly 10cm long.

Cook the Koftas
Heat a griddle pan (or a regular frying pan if that's all you've got) over medium-high heat. Cook the koftas for about 6-8 minutes, turning them regularly until browned on all sides. Set the cooked koftas to one side.

Simmer the Spicy Tomato Sauce
In the same pan, heat the olive oil in a pan over medium heat, then toss in the garlic and fry for about 30 seconds until fragrant (but not burnt). Pour in the tomatoes, harissa, sugar, and a pinch of salt and pepper. Let it bubble away uncovered for 15-20 minutes, stirring now and then, until thickened.

Return the koftas to the sauce and let them warm through.

Serve and Enjoy
Spoon the sauce onto a warm plate, drizzle over the yogurt, and lay the koftas on top. Serve with warm pittas or a generous helping of couscous.

Moroccan Lamb Mini Burgers

These flavorful Moroccan lamb sliders pack a punch with bold spices and a cooling harissa yogurt sauce. They're quick, easy, and made entirely in your RidgeMonkey sandwich toaster.

Prep: 10 minutes, Cook: 10 mins Servings: 4

Equipment

RidgeMonkey sandwich toaster (or a standard pan)
Small mixing bowl
Plate for mixing spices

Ingredients

250g (1/2 lb) ground lamb
1/2 tbsp Ras el Hanout
1/4 tsp salt
2 tbsp Greek yogurt
1/2 tbsp harissa
Juice of 1/4 lemon
1 tsp olive oil
4 small slider buns, split
4 fresh mint leaves (for garnish)

How to make it

Prepare the Harissa Yogurt Sauce
In a small bowl, mix the Greek yogurt, harissa, lemon juice, a pinch of salt, and olive oil until smooth. Set aside for topping.

Season the Lamb
On a plate, mix the Ras el Hanout and a big pinch of salt. Divide the ground lamb into 4 equal portions and shape each into a small patty about the size of your slider buns. Coat each patty lightly in the spice mixture.

Cook the Patties
Preheat your RidgeMonkey sandwich toaster over medium heat. Lightly oil the toaster plates if necessary. Place the patties inside, close the toaster, and cook for about 3-4 minutes per side, or until browned and cooked through.

Toast the Buns
Remove the patties and place the slider buns inside the toaster to lightly toast for about 1-2 minutes.

Assemble the Sliders
Spread a dollop of the harissa yogurt on the bottom half of each bun. Add a lamb patty, top with a mint leaf, and place the other half of the bun on top. Or if you're greedy like me, double them up with 2 patties!

Serve
Serve warm and enjoy!

Shakshuka

Totally my favourite breakfast on a cold morning in the van! It's packed with smoky spices, slow-simmered tomatoes, and perfectly poached eggs. Soak up that flavour with some crusty bread!

Prep: 10 minutes, Cook: 25 mins Servings: 2

Equipment

Large frying pan with lid
Chopping board & knife
Wooden spoon
Small bowl

Ingredients

1 tbsp olive oil
1 onion, finely chopped
1 red pepper, diced
2 cloves garlic, minced
1 tsp ground cumin
1 tsp smoked paprika
½ tsp dried oregano
¼ tsp cayenne pepper (optional, but adds a nice kick)
1 small red chilli, finely chopped
1 tin (400g) chopped tomatoes
Salt & black pepper, to taste
4 eggs
Fresh coriander, for garnish
Crusty bread or flatbread, to serve

How to make it

Heat the olive oil in a large frying pan over medium heat. Add the onion and cook until soft and translucent, about 5 minutes. Toss in the red pepper and cook for another 3 minutes.

Stir in the garlic, cumin, smoked paprika, oregano, cayenne (if using), and chopped chilli. Cook for 1-2 minutes until fragrant.

Pour in the chopped tomatoes and season with salt and black pepper. Let it bubble away for 10 minutes, stirring occasionally, until slightly thickened.

Make four small wells in the sauce and crack an egg into each. Cover with a lid and let them cook for about 5-7 minutes, or until the whites are set but the yolks are still runny.

Sprinkle with fresh coriander, then grab some crusty bread and dig in straight from the pan.

Preserved Lemons

Preserved lemons are a tangy, salty flavor bomb that adds depth to everything from stews to salads. This simple recipe uses just lemons, salt, and their own juice to create a next level exciting layer of flavour to your dish.

Prep: 15 minutes, Preserve Time: 3 weeks

Equipment

Sterilized jar with a tight-fitting lid (about 500ml capacity)
Sharp knife
Cutting board

Ingredients

4 medium unwaxed lemons
1/4 cup (60g) coarse salt
Freshly squeezed lemon juice (from about 2 additional lemons)

How to make it

Prepare the Lemons
Wash and scrub the lemons thoroughly to remove any wax or residue. Cut a deep cross into each lemon, starting from the top and stopping about 1cm from the base so the quarters remain attached.

Salt the Lemons
Open the cut lemons slightly and pack the inside with coarse salt, about 1 tablespoon per lemon.

Pack the Jar
Place a layer of salt at the bottom of the sterilized jar. Pack the lemons into the jar as tightly as possible, sprinkling a little extra salt between layers. Press down firmly to release the lemon juice.

Add Lemon Juice
Squeeze the juice from the additional lemons and pour it over the salted lemons until they are completely submerged.

Seal and Store
Seal the jar tightly and leave it at room temperature for 2-3 days, shaking the jar gently each day to distribute the salt and juices. After that, store the jar in a cool, dark place or the fridge for at least 3 weeks before using.

Notes
Flavour Boost: For extra aromatics, tuck in a bay leaf, cinnamon stick, or a few whole peppercorns before sealing the jar.
Shelf Life: Once opened, preserved lemons will keep in the fridge for up to 6 months if submerged in their brine.
Use these citrusy gems in tagines, salad dressings, or anywhere you need a zesty punch of flavor!

Moroccan-Inspired Chicken "No" Tagine

You can't beat a beautiful tagine simmering away, but the flavours from this recipe will fill your van with the essence of Morocco, and I guarantee you'll be salivating while waiting to dive into this meal!

Prep: 10 minutes, Cook: 35 mins Servings: 2

Equipment

Non-stick skillet with a lid
Mixing spoon
Cutting board and knife

Ingredients

2 small onions, chopped
2 tbsp chopped parsley (plus extra for garnish)
1 tbsp olive oil (plus more for drizzling)
350g chicken breast or thigh, diced
1/2 tsp ground ginger
1/4 tsp ground turmeric
1/4 tsp ground cumin
1/4 preserved lemon, finely, chopped - **See page 71**
Salt and black pepper, to taste
1/4 cup (40g) pitted olives

How to make it

Cook the Onions
Heat olive oil in a non-stick skillet over medium heat. Add the chopped onions and parsley, cooking for 3-4 minutes until the onions become soft and translucent.

Add the Chicken and Spices
Stir in the diced chicken, ground ginger, turmeric, cumin, preserved lemon, salt, and pepper. Mix well to coat the chicken evenly in the spices.

Simmer the Stew
Add 1-2 tablespoons of water, cover the skillet, and lower the heat to medium-low. Let the mixture simmer for 20-25 minutes, stirring occasionally, until the chicken is tender and the onions have fully cooked down.

Add the Olives
Stir in the olives about 5 minutes before the stew is done. Cover again and allow the flavors to meld.

Finish and Serve
Once the chicken is cooked through, remove from heat. Garnish with additional parsley and a drizzle of olive oil.

Notes
Shortcut: Use store-bought preserved lemons to save prep time.
Extra Flavor: Add a pinch of chilli flakes for a subtle kick

A little preserved lemon goes a long way, and this dish will take your taste buds straight to the markets of Morocco. Enjoy!

SOUTH AMERICA

In Peru, you can get a burger made from a giant Amazonian worm that looks like it crawled out of Jurassic Park. It's grilled up on skewers and even slapped into buns like a juicy burger. Locals swear it's buttery, protein-packed, and a natural energy booster... but tourists? They usually just scream and run.

Choripán Inspired Hot Dog

A no-fuss, full-flavour street food classic straight from Argentina and Uruguay. Choripán is all about smoky, juicy chorizo stuffed into a warm, crusty roll. It's a simple, satisfying, and delicious alternative to a hot dog.

Prep: 2 minutes, Cook: 10 mins Servings: 2

Equipment

Frying pan or skillet
Knife & cutting board
Tongs or spatula

Ingredients

2 chorizo sausages (or any smoky, spicy sausage)
2 crusty rolls (baguette, ciabatta, or whatever you've got)
½ tablespoon oil for frying
Chimichuri **see page 79**

How to make it

Cook the Chorizo
Heat a pan over medium heat with a little oil. Slice the sausages in half lengthwise (without cutting all the way through) and press them flat. Fry for about 4-5 minutes per side until browned and slightly crispy.

Toast the Bread
If space allows, place the rolls cut-side down in the pan for a minute or two until warm and slightly crisp.

Assemble & Serve
Stuff the sausages into the bread and enjoy as is, or add your favourite sauce–mayo, mustard, or that chimichurri you've already made from page 79.

Argentinian Steak Sandwich

Steak, cheese and fresh chimichurri...come on! The steak and cheese is a classic, but with the fresh chimichurri it comes to life with a vibrant zing that sings to your taste buds!

Prep: 10 minutes, Cook: 10 mins Servings: 2 (or 1 big one)

Equipment

Frying pan or skillet
Tongs
Knife & cutting board
Small bowl

Ingredients

1 ribeye steak
1 small onion, sliced
1 ciabatta loaf (or two small ciabatta rolls)
2 slices of cheese (cheddar, provolone, or whatever melts nicely)
2 tbsp chimichurri **see page 79**
1 tbsp olive oil
½ tbsp butter
Salt & black pepper, to taste

How to make it

Fry the Onions
Heat half the olive oil and butter in a pan over medium heat. Toss in the sliced onions with a pinch of salt and cook until soft, golden, and slightly caramelised (about 5-7 minutes). Set aside.

Cook the Steak
Season the ribeye generously with salt and black pepper. Add the remaining oil to the pan and bring it to high heat. Sear the steak for about 2-3 minutes per side (for medium-rare) or longer if you prefer. Rest for 5 minutes, then slice thinly.

Toast the Bread
While the steak rests, slice the ciabatta and toast it lightly in the same pan with all the meat juices and add a bit of butter until golden and crisp.

Assemble the Sandwich
Lay the steak slices over the bottom half of the ciabatta, followed by the fried onions and cheese. If your pan is still warm, pop the whole thing back in for a minute with the lid on to help melt the cheese.

Finishing Touch
Slather the top half of the ciabatta with a generous spoonful of chimichurri, then press everything together. Slice in half and devour immediately.

Authentic Chimichurri

In my opinion, there should be a tub of this Argentinian gold in your fridge indefinitely! A punchy, herby sauce that takes any meal from "meh" to mouthwatering. Perfect for drizzling over grilled meats.

Servings: 2 | Prep Time: 5 minutes | Rest Time: 10+ minutes

Equipment

Small bowl
Manual Blender
Spoon for stirring

Ingredients

½ cup (120ml) olive oil
2 tbsp red wine vinegar
¾ tsp dried oregano
½ cup (30g) fresh parsley, finely chopped
3-4 garlic cloves, minced
1 small red chilli (or ½ tsp dried chilli flakes), finely chopped
1 tsp coarse salt
½ tsp black pepper

How to make it

Chuck everything into the blender and give it a good blend.

Let it sit for at least 10 minutes–this gives the flavours a chance to blend. Ideally, leave it for a couple of hours (or overnight in the fridge) for an even bolder taste.

Spoon generously over grilled steak, chicken, or roasted veggies.

You can easily freeze Chimichurri for use at a later date. Consider an extra large ice cube tray to portion it out.

South American Arepas

Arepas have officially become my culinary BFF! Late-night munchies? Check! Breakfast boost? You bet! Lunch delight? Absolutely! These little pockets of joy are so easy and versatile, they play nice with anything, anytime!

Prep: 5 minutes, Cook: 10 mins Servings: 4 Arepas

Equipment

Mixing bowl
Measuring cups
Fork or hands for mixing
Non-stick pan or skillet
Spatula

Ingredients

1 cup pre-cooked cornmeal (masarepa)
1 cup warm water
1 tsp salt
1 tsp butter (plus extra for cooking)

How to make it

Make the Dough

In a bowl, mix the warm water and salt. Gradually add the cornmeal, stirring with a fork or your hands until it forms a soft, pliable dough. Let it sit for 2 minutes so the cornmeal absorbs the liquid.

Shape the Arepas

Knead the dough for a minute, then divide it into two equal portions. Roll each into a ball and gently flatten into discs about ½-inch thick.
Make sure the Arepas are flat and not bulging as they will not cook evenly.

Cook

Heat a little butter in a pan over medium heat. Cook the arepas for about 5 minutes on each side, pressing them down slightly with a spatula, until they develop a golden crust.

Serve

Slice open and fill with cheese, beans, avocado, or anything delicious you have lying around. Or just slather them in butter and call it a day.

Try this:

- Grate some Parmesan cheese into the dough to make the Arepas extra cheesy.
- Make a dip in the uncooked dough and sandwich some mozzarella in the middle for a rich, gooey middle when pulled apart.

RidgeMonkey

Caribbean Lamb Curry

Jerked meat is pretty legendary at any BBQ, and this recipe takes all of those Jamaican flavours into an unbelievably tasty lamb curry. I'm salivating just thinking about the taste of this!

Prep: 45 minutes, Cook: 30 mins Servings: 2-4

Equipment

Non-stick skillet with a lid
Mixing spoon
Cutting board and knife

Ingredients

350g lamb, diced
1 onion, chopped
1 tsp vinegar
2 garlic cloves, crushed
1 tsp freshly grated ginger
1 small scotch bonnet pepper, seeds removed and finely chopped
1 tsp allspice
1 tsp ground cumin
1 tsp turmeric
1 tsp ground ginger
1 tsp ground coriander
1/2 tsp fenugreek seeds
1/2 tsp salt
1 spring onion, chopped
1 sprig of fresh thyme
1 small carrot, chopped
1 small potato, diced
1 tbsp cooking oil
400ml coconut milk
200g green beans, trimmed
1 lime, juiced

How to make it

Marinate the Lamb
In a large bowl, combine the diced lamb, vinegar, onion, garlic, scotch bonnet pepper, allspice, ginger, salt, and all the spices. Mix thoroughly, ensuring the lamb is well coated. Give it a jerk! You don't have to but it's fun to! Cover and marinade for at least 30 minutes (or longer for more intense flavor).

Brown the Lamb
Heat the cooking oil in a skillet over medium heat. Add the marinated lamb and stir well. Cook until the lamb is lightly browned on all sides, about 5-7 minutes. Add a splash of water if the pan gets too dry.

Add Vegetables and Coconut Milk
Stir in the carrot, potato, and thyme. Pour in enough coconut milk to cover the lamb and vegetables. Stir well and bring to a gentle simmer.

Cook the Curry
Cover the skillet and let the curry cook for 25-30 minutes, stirring occasionally, until the lamb is fully cooked, the vegetables are tender, and the liquid has reduced into a rich, flavorful gravy.

Finish and Serve
Add the green beans during the last 5 minutes of cooking to keep them crisp. Squeeze in the lime juice just before serving for a fresh, tangy finish. Garnish with the sliced spring onion.

Serve with rice or bread. I like to eat it with rice and peas.

NORTH AMERICA

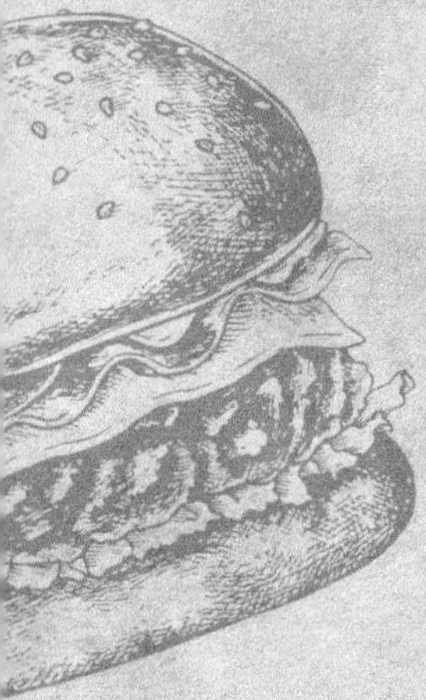

In the U.S., there's a taco so spicy, it has sent people straight to the ER.

Meet the "Diablo Death Taco", a street taco from New York loaded with ghost pepper sauce so lethal, diners have signed waivers before eating it.

Don't worry it's not in this book!

Coriander Crema

This is a simple sauce that I tend to use for so many things. Even if it is just on eggs! Here are some ways in which you can use it to bring dishes to life:

Tacos & Wraps

- Drizzle over fish tacos, beef burritos, or veggie wraps for a creamy, tangy kick.
- Use it as a spread for quesadillas or enchiladas.

Grilled Meats & Seafood

- Serve alongside grilled chicken, steak, or shrimp as a flavorful dipping sauce.
- Spoon it over roasted or grilled fish for an herby boost.

Bowls & Salads

- Add it to grain bowls with quinoa, rice, or farro, along with roasted veggies and proteins.
- Use it as a salad dressing for a fresh, vibrant taste.

Burgers & Sandwiches

- Spread on buns for burgers or sliders, especially with Mexican-inspired flavours.
- Layer into deli sandwiches for an herby twist.

Snacks & Appetizers

- Serve as a dip for tortilla chips, veggie sticks, or potato wedges.
- Top nachos or loaded fries with a generous drizzle.

Egg Dishes

- Spoon over scrambled eggs, omelettes, or frittatas.
- Drizzle on breakfast burritos or huevos rancheros.

Soups & Stews

- Swirl into black bean soup, tortilla soup, or lentil stew for a creamy garnish.

Other Creative Ideas

- Use it as a base sauce for pizza with chicken, avocado, or roasted veggies.
- Mix into mashed potatoes or polenta for extra flavor.

Coriander crema's balance of creaminess and herby brightness makes it a winner on so many dishes–basically, if you love it, put it on everything!

Prep: 5 minutes, Cook: 0 mins Servings: Half a cup

Equipment

Small blender or food processor

Ingredients

4 tbsp sour cream
A small handful of fresh coriander (roughly chopped)
Salt and black pepper, to taste

How to make it

Combine the sour cream and coriander in a small blender or food processor. Blend until smooth.

Season with salt and black pepper to taste.

Serve immediately or refrigerate until ready to use.

Chicken Taquitos

These resemble rolled tacos that you can enjoy without any mess while you crunch away. They combine all the delicious flavours and textures of a taco, offering a delightful bite akin to that of a spring roll. They also make for a fantastic option for leftovers!

Prep: 10 minutes, Cook: 10 mins Servings: 4 Taquitos

Equipment

Large mixing bowl
Medium frying pan
Tongs or slotted spoon
Wooden toothpicks
Paper towels

Ingredients

200g (about 1 cup) boneless, skinless chicken breast, finely diced
2 diced green chillies
50g mature cheddar cheese, grated
50g mozzarella cheese, grated
¼ cup chopped fresh coriander
1 tsp chilli powder
½ tsp ground cumin
Pinch of salt
A splash of hot sauce (adjust to taste)
4 flour or corn tortillas (15cm diameter), warmed
Oil for frying (around 1/2 cups, depending on pan size)
Coriander Crema **See page 85**

How to make it

Prepare the Chicken Mixture
Heat a drizzle of oil in a frying pan over medium heat. Add the diced chicken, chilli powder, cumin, and a pinch of salt, cooking for 5-7 minutes until the chicken is fully cooked and lightly browned. Stir in the green chillies and cook for another minute to combine the flavours.

Mix with Cheese and Herbs
Once the chicken is cooked, transfer it to a bowl. Let it cool slightly, then mix in the mature cheddar, mozzarella, and fresh coriander. Add a splash of hot sauce and stir until everything is evenly combined.

Assemble the Taquitos
Lay a tortilla flat on a clean surface. Scoop about ⅓ cup of the chicken mixture into the centre. Roll it up tightly, starting from the bottom, and secure the seam with a toothpick. Repeat for the remaining tortillas.

Fry them up
Add the oil to the pan and heat. Place the taquitos in and toast on each side until golden brown. Be careful - they burn easily!

Load up a plate
Place all the taquitos on a plate and pile on some more cheese, salsa and coriander crema see page 85.

Enjoy!

Honey Garlic Chicken

Sticky, sweet, and savoury chicken bites coated in a golden honey-garlic glaze, brightened with a splash of citrus and fresh spring onion. A street food treat that's easy to whip up in any tiny kitchen!

Prep: 5 minutes, Cook: 10 mins Servings: 2

Equipment

Cutting board and knife
Bowl for mixing
Frying pan
Wooden spoon

Ingredients

For the Chicken
350g chicken breast, diced into bite-sized pieces
1 tsp salt
1 tsp black pepper
2 tbsp all-purpose flour

For the Sauce
2 tbsp honey
1 tbsp soy sauce
1 tbsp vinegar (white or apple cider)
15g (0.5 oz) butter
3-5 garlic cloves, minced

Optional Garnishes
Zest and juice of ½ orange
1-2 spring onions, finely sliced

How to make it

Prep the Chicken
Toss the diced chicken in a bowl with salt, pepper, and flour until evenly coated.

Cook the Chicken
Heat a frying pan over medium heat and melt the butter. Once sizzling, add the chicken pieces and cook until golden and crispy on the outside and cooked through, about 5-7 minutes. Remove and set aside.

Make the Sauce
In the same pan, lower the heat and add the garlic, stirring until fragrant (about 30 seconds). Add honey, soy sauce, and vinegar, stirring to combine. Let the sauce simmer and thicken slightly, about 1-2 minutes.

Coat the Chicken
Return the cooked chicken to the pan, tossing to coat each piece in the sticky honey garlic glaze. Let the sauce start to bubble in darken (but don't let it burn!)

Add a Citrus Twist (Optional)
For a burst of freshness, stir in the juice of half an orange and sprinkle in some zest.

Serve
Plate the chicken bites and garnish with thinly sliced spring onions. Pair with rice, noodles, or eat straight out of the pan for a casual treat.

Timeless Tacos

There's so many types of tacos, but lets face it, the OG is always going to be soft tortillas filled with juicy, seared steak, gooey melted cheese, and a kick of spice.

Prep: 10 minutes, Cook: 15 mins Servings: 2

Equipment

Frying pan or griddle
Tongs
Sharp knife
Small bowl
Chopping board

Ingredients

150g (5 oz) steak (ribeye or sirloin works best)
1/2 tsp smoked paprika
1/2 tsp ground cumin
Salt & black pepper, to taste
1/2 tbsp olive oil
2 small flour or corn tortillas
30g (1 oz) grated cheddar cheese (or Monterey Jack)
1/4 small red onion, finely chopped
1/2 lime, cut into wedges
1/4 small bunch fresh coriander (cilantro), chopped
1/2 small jalapeño, finely sliced (optional, for heat)
1 tbsp sour cream or Greek yoghurt or Coriander Crema, **see page 85**

How to make it

Season the Steak
Pat the steak dry with a paper towel. Rub it all over with smoked paprika, cumin, salt, and black pepper. Let it sit while you prep the toppings–this gives the spices a chance to work their magic.

Sear the Steak
Heat a frying pan over medium-high heat and add the olive oil. Once it's hot, slap the steak in the pan and let it sear for about 2-3 minutes per side, depending on how you like it cooked. Remove from the pan and let it rest for a couple of minutes before slicing it into thin strips.

Warm the Tortillas
While the steak rests, toss the tortillas into the still-hot pan for about 30 seconds per side until they're warm and slightly charred in spots.

Assemble the Tacos
Lay out the tortillas and sprinkle the cheese over them so it starts melting slightly from the warmth. Top with the steak slices, red onion, and a handful of fresh coriander. If you're a spice lover, throw on some jalapeño slices.

Final Touches
Drizzle a bit of sour cream or coriander crema over the top and serve with lime wedges on the side. Give everything a squeeze of fresh lime before digging in.

Burrito Tacos

A taco and a burrito had a love child, and it's as glorious as it sounds. These burrito tacos are a delightful fusion of flavours and textures, bringing together the best of both worlds in one delicious bite.

Prep: 10 minutes, Cook: 15 mins Servings: 2

Equipment

Frying pan
Small saucepan
Knife & chopping board
Small bowl
Fork

Ingredients

2 small flour or corn tortillas
80g (½ cup) cooked rice (white or brown)
½ tbsp olive oil
½ tsp smoked paprika
½ tsp ground cumin
½ tsp garlic powder
½ tin (120g) black beans, drained and rinsed
1/4 small red onion, finely chopped
Salt & black pepper, to taste
Handful of shredded lettuce
1 tbsp soured cream (or coriander crema from **page 85**)
1/4 small bunch fresh coriander (cilantro), chopped
1/2 lime, cut into wedges

How to make it

Cook the Rice
If you don't already have cooked rice, get that sorted first. In a small saucepan, add ½ cup of water, a pinch of salt, and the rice. Simmer until the water is absorbed and the rice is tender. Fluff it up with a fork and set aside.

Sauté the Beans
Heat olive oil in a frying pan over medium heat. Toss in the black beans, red onion, smoked paprika, cumin, garlic powder, salt, and black pepper. Stir and let everything cook for about 3-4 minutes until warmed through and slightly crispy in spots.

Warm the Tortillas
While the beans do their thing, chuck the tortillas into a dry pan for about 30 seconds per side until warm and slightly golden.

Assemble the Burrito Tacos
Divide the cooked rice between the tortillas, spreading it out slightly. Pile on the seasoned black beans, then scatter over the shredded lettuce.

Final Touches
Top with a generous spoonful of soured cream (or coriander crema) and a sprinkle of fresh coriander. Serve with lime wedges and squeeze over some juice before taking a bite.

Avo’cuddle Breakfast

Who needs a fancy brunch when you can whip up this ridiculously good breakfast right on your stovetop? Crispy tortilla chips, creamy avocado, smoky black beans, and a perfectly fried egg.

Prep: 5 minutes, Cook: 10 mins Servings: 2

Equipment

Frying pan
Small saucepan
Knife
Chopping board
Spatula

Ingredients

2 small tortillas
½ avocado, sliced
2 eggs
80g black beans (about ½ cup), drained
40g feta cheese (about ⅓ cup), crumbled
1 tbsp oil
½ tsp smoked paprika
Salt & pepper to taste

How to make it

Make the Chips
Heat half the oil in a frying pan over medium heat. Cut the tortillas into triangles and toast them in the pan until golden and crispy, flipping halfway through. Set aside.

Cook the Black Beans
In a small saucepan, heat the remaining oil over low heat. Add the black beans, smoked paprika, and a pinch of salt. Stir and let them sizzle for 2-3 minutes until warmed through.

Fry the Eggs
In the same pan used for the tortillas, crack in the eggs and fry to your liking–crispy edges are encouraged.

Assemble & Serve
Pile the tortilla chips onto plates. Spoon over the warm black beans, top with fried eggs, and scatter the sliced avocado and crumbled feta on top. Finish with a sprinkle of black pepper.

Pro Tip: Feeling extra fancy? A dash of hot sauce or a squeeze of lime takes this to another level.

Cast Iron Skillet Corn on the Cob with Lime and Chilli

This adaptation of the classic street food brings out the smoky, charred flavors of grilled corn but is perfectly suited for cooking in a cast iron skillet on the stovetop or over a portable camping stove.

Prep: 5 minutes, Cook: 10 mins Servings: 2

Equipment

Cast iron skillet
Small bowl

Ingredients

3 corn on the cobs
3/4 tsp salt
1/4 tsp chilli powder (adjust to taste)
1 1/2 limes, halved

How to make it

Prepare the Corn
Peel the husks and silks from the corn cobs. If needed, cut the corn in half to fit your skillet.

Heat the Skillet
Place the cast iron skillet over medium-high heat. Once hot, add the corn cobs directly to the dry skillet. No oil is necessary.

Char the Corn
Cook the corn for about 10 minutes, turning every 2-3 minutes. Allow the kernels to develop a charred, golden-brown appearance on all sides.

Prepare the Lime Mixture
In a small bowl, mix the salt and chilli powder. Dip the cut side of each lime half into the salt-chilli mixture, pressing lightly to coat.

Season the Corn
Once the corn is cooked, remove it from the skillet. Immediately rub the cut, seasoned lime halves over the hot corn, squeezing the lime as you go to infuse the corn with its salty, spicy, and tangy flavors.

Serve Hot
Serve the corn fresh off the skillet while it's still warm. Adjust the seasoning if needed and enjoy.

Fiery Salsa

This is yet another essential condiment to know as it adds zing and crunch to so many dishes. It's worthy of space in our tiny fridges!

Toppings and Dips

- Tacos & Burritos - Add to your favourite tacos, burritos, or enchiladas for a burst of fresh flavour.
- Chips & Dips - Serve as a classic dip for tortilla chips or alongside guacamole.

Breakfast Ideas

- Eggs - Spoon over scrambled eggs, poached eggs, or an omelette.
- Breakfast Bowls - Use it as a topper for breakfast bowls with hash browns, avocado, and bacon.
- Huevos Rancheros - Pair it with fried eggs, black beans, and tortillas.

Bowls & Mains

- Grain Bowls - Add to rice, quinoa, or farro bowls with roasted veggies and grilled protein.
- Grilled Meat or Fish - Use as a sauce for grilled chicken, pork, steak, or fish for a fresh, zesty touch.

Snacks & Appetisers

- Loaded Nachos - Drizzle over nachos along with melted cheese, sour cream, and jalapeños.
- Mini Toast or Crostini - Spread on small toast with a layer of cream cheese or smashed avocado.

Salads & Wraps

- Salad Dressing - Mix with olive oil and lime juice for a vibrant salad dressing.
- Wraps & Sandwiches - Spread inside wraps or sandwiches for a fresh kick.

Cooking Enhancements

- Marinade or Sauce - Use as a marinade for meats or veggies or a simmering sauce for quick sautés.
- Pasta or Rice - Stir into pasta, rice, or grain dishes for added zest.

Prep: 5 minutes, Cook: 0 mins Servings: 1 cup

Equipment

Small blender or food processor

Ingredients

1 small onion, roughly chopped
1-2 fresh chillies, deseeded for less heat (optional)
1 small handful of fresh coriander
1 tsp apple cider vinegar
2 medium tomatoes, diced
Salt and black pepper, to taste

How to make it

Blend the Base
Combine the onion, chillies, coriander, and cider vinegar in a small blender or food processor. Blitz until smooth.

Add Tomatoes
Stir in the diced tomatoes for texture.

Season
Add salt and pepper to taste, adjusting as needed.

Tex-Mex Brekkie

Just when you thought a British classic of bacon and eggs was unbeatable the Texans swoop in and turn up the heat with their spicy twist!

Prep: 10 minutes, Cook: 20 mins Servings: 2

Equipment

Cutting board and knife
Frying pan
Small blender or food processor
Medium saucepan
Wooden spoon
Whisk

Ingredients

Coriander Crema, **see page 85**
Fiery Salsa, see **page 99**

For the Polenta Mash
½ cup quick-cooking polenta (about 85g)
2 cups water (480ml)
⅓ cup shredded cheese (cheddar or a Tex-Mex blend works great)
1 tsp hot sauce
Salt and black pepper, to taste

For the Main Dish
4 slices streaky bacon
2 eggs
1 large potato, cut into small cubes

How to make it

Cook the Potato
Heat a frying pan over medium heat and add the small potato cubes and let them fry evenly for 5 minutes.

Add the Bacon
To the same pan add the bacon and fry until crispy, flipping as needed. Once done, transfer everything to a paper towel to drain excess grease.

Make the Polenta Mash
In a saucepan, bring the water to a boil with a pinch of salt. Gradually whisk in the polenta, stirring constantly to avoid lumps. Reduce the heat and cook for 3-5 minutes until thickened. Stir in the cheese, hot sauce, and a good grind of black pepper. Keep warm.

Cook the Eggs
In the same pan used for the bacon (because fewer dishes = happiness), fry or scramble the eggs to your liking.

Assemble the Dish
Divide the polenta between two plates, spreading it out as a base. Top with the potato, crispy bacon slices and eggs. Drizzle with the coriander crema and finish with a generous dollop of salsa.

Cheesy Chilli Con Carne

This warm, cheesy chilli is just perfect! The Omnia is perfect for cooking without a traditional oven and this bake will show you why. It's a comforting one-pot meal that's packed with flavor and ideal for sharing. Serve it up with tortilla chips for scooping and crunching!

Prep: 5 minutes, Cook: 45 mins Servings: 2

Equipment

Omnia stove-top oven
Medium mixing spoon
Cutting board and knife

Ingredients

1 tbsp olive oil
2 garlic cloves, minced
1 small onion, diced
1 red bell pepper, diced
400g ground beef (mince)
1 1/2 tbsp tomato paste
200g canned crushed tomatoes (half a standard can)
400g red kidney beans, drained
1 beef stock cube, crumbled
1/2 cup of hot water
1/2 tsp sugar
Salt and pepper, to taste
1 cup shredded cheddar cheese
Tortilla chips, for serving

Chilli Spice Mix:
1 tsp cayenne pepper (adjust to taste)
2 tsp paprika powder
2 tsp cumin powder
2 tsp dried oregano

How to make it

Preheat the Omnia Oven
Place the Omnia oven on high heat for a few minutes to preheat while prepping ingredients.

Cook the Base
Add olive oil to the Omnia, followed by garlic and onion. Sauté for 1 minute, then add the diced bell pepper. Cook for another 2 minutes until the onion turns translucent.

Brown the Beef
Add the ground beef to the pan. Use a spoon to break it apart as it cooks, until mostly browned.

Spice It Up
Sprinkle the chilli spice mix over the beef and stir to coat. Cover the Omnia with its lid and let the beef finish browning evenly, about 2 minutes.

Simmer the Chilli
Stir in the tomato paste, crushed tomatoes, kidney beans, crumbled stock cube, hot water, sugar, and a pinch of salt and pepper. Add half the cheddar cheese and stir it into the mix and the remaining half sprinkled on top. Lower the heat slightly and bring the chilli to a gentle simmer, covering the Omnia with its lid. Let it cook for 45 minutes.

Taste and Serve
This one is perfect for sharing so wedge in some tortilla chips and get scooping and munching.

EUROPE

In Italy, eating pizza with a fork is basically considered a crime —but in Naples, if your slice flops, it's called a "cornicione morto" (dead crust).
So if your pizza's limp... well, let's just say, it's not impressing anyone.

Neapolitan Ragu

Rich, slow-cooked tomato sauce meets tender, flavour-packed meat–this is Naples-style ragu at its best. It's one of those dishes that gently simmers away, making your van smell like an Italian trattoria. Serve the sauce with pasta and save the meat for main.

Prep: 15 minutes, Cook: 2 Hours+, Servings: plenty!

Equipment

Large saucepan or deep frying pan with a lid
Wooden spoon
Chopping board & knife

Ingredients

1 small onion, finely chopped
1 small carrot, finely chopped
1 celery stick, finely chopped
200g beef (or any meat you fancy)
200g pork (optional–mix it up!)
A splash of red wine (about 60ml)
1 tin (400g) chopped or crushed tomatoes
1 tbsp tomato purée
½ tsp salt, or to taste
½ tsp sugar (balances the acidity)
1 small handful fresh basil leaves
1 tbsp olive oil

How to make it

Start with the Soffritto
Heat the olive oil in your pan over medium heat. Add the onion, carrot, and celery. Cook gently for about 5 minutes, stirring occasionally, until soft and fragrant. This is your flavour base–don't rush it!

Brown the Meat
Heat a splash of oil in your pan over medium heat. Add your chosen meat and brown it on all sides. You're not cooking it through, just giving it some colour.

Deglaze with Wine
Pour in the red wine and let it bubble away for a minute, scraping up any delicious bits from the bottom. No wine? No stress–just skip it.

Add the Tomatoes
Tip in the chopped tomatoes and stir in the tomato purée.

Season and Simmer
Sprinkle in the salt, a tiny bit of sugar (trust me, it balances the acidity), and tear in the fresh basil. Give it a stir, then cover with the lid slightly ajar.

Low and Slow
Let it simmer gently for at least 2 hours, stirring occasionally to stop it catching on the bottom. Keep the heat low–you want a lazy, slow bubble, not a rolling boil.

Serve it Up
Spoon the rich, thick sauce over pasta. The meat? Set it aside for tomorrow's meal, or enjoy it now with some veggies.

Fritto Misto

Fritto Misto is a crispy, golden seafood delight that's synonymous with the coastal towns of Italy, particularly along the Amalfi Coast. In Italy, you'll find this served in paper cones for snacking on the go, or as a main course at seaside trattorias.

Prep: 5 minutes, Cook: 6-8 minutes, Servings: 2

Equipment

Gas stove
Large, deep frying pan
Slotted spoon
Cutting board
Knife
1 Small bowl
1 Dinner plate

Ingredients

1 red onion, thinly sliced
3 tbsp of apple cider vinegar
1/2 cup of 00 flour
1/2 tsp of salt
1/2 tsp of pepper
1 1/2 cups of raw mixed seafood
2 cup of cherry tomatoes
1 large lemon, sliced (save the ends)
2 cups of vegetable oil
1/2 cup of fresh parsley

How to make it

Start by placing the thinly sliced red onion in a small bowl and mix in the apple cider vinegar. Leave this to one side and watch the colour change to a vibrant purple.

Pour the oil into a deep frying pan and turn up to a high'ish heat.

Scatter the flour on the dinner plate and toss in the seafood and the lemon slices. Make sure it is all thoroughly coated.

Check the heat of the oil by dropping in a small pinch of flour. You want it to sizzle on the surface to know it is ready.

Fry the flour coated seafood, cherry tomatoes and lemon slices in 2 batches ensuring the flour coated seafood turns golden before removing from the oil.

Season the seafood and lemon heavily with salt and pepper and squeeze over the fried lemon ends.

Serve with the vibrant pickled red onion and a garnish of fresh parsley.

Tips

Be careful with the hot oil. Do not overcrowd the pan and ensure you have a tidy cooking area and a well ventilated campervan! It is also advised to have a damp tea towel to one side should you get in to trouble with any fire.
Serve on a platter and let everyone pick away!

RidgeMonkey

Meatball Bruschetta

Juicy, well-seasoned meatballs perched on crisp slices of toasted baguette, slathered in a rich tomato sauce, and finished with a generous sprinkle of parmesan and fresh basil.

Prep: 10 minutes, Cook: 2 hours, Servings: 15 meatballs

Equipment

Mixing bowl
Frying pan

Ingredients

For the meatballs
ground beef mince How much?
ground pork mince
1 egg, beaten
sultanas
1 small onion, finely chopped
breadcrumbs
parmigiano reggiano, grated
1 tbsp cocoa powder
1 tsp salt

For the ragu
1 tbsp lard
1 small onion, finely chopped
1 tbsp tomato puree
500g tomato passata
1 tbsp sugar
1 cup of fresh basil
1/2 cup red wine

For the bruschetta
sliced bread of your choice
shredded mozzarella
olive oil

How to make it

In your mixing bowl add the ground beef and the ground pork and season with quite a lot of salt.

Add the finely chopped onion, the chopped sultanas, the breadcrumbs, cocoa powder, the egg and the grated Parmigiano Reggiano.

Time to get your hands messy! Mix everything together by squeezing it all in your hands. Make sure everything is incorporated into a well mixed ball of meat.

Divide the meat into about 15 portions and form into ping pong ball sized balls. DO NOT roll them too tightly as this will make them dense and less juicy.

In a saucepan add the lard and a chopped onion and cook on a medium/high heat until fragrant and soft.

Push the onion to the side to make space in the middle of the pan and carefully add the meatballs and brown them. Keep them moving and sizzling in the pan for 3 minutes. This is to add flavour to the pan.

Pour in 1/2 cup of red wine and deglaze the bottom of the pan. Wait until the wine has evaporated and then add the passata, the tomato puree, fresh basil, salt and sugar and give it all a good mix and cook on a very low simmer for 2 hours.

In the meantime toast up some slices of bread and drizzle with olive oil and top with shredded mozzarella.

Serve the meatballs upon the cheesy bruschetta drenched in the ragu and topped with fresh basil.

Beef Braciole

Beef Braciole is a classic Italian dish featuring thinly tenderised beef rolled with a flavorful filling of breadcrumbs, cheese, prosciutto and herbs. Simmered in a rich tomato sauce, offering tender beef infused with robust Mediterranean flavours. Wait for the smell to fill your kitchen!

Prep: 10 minutes, Cook: 1 hour, Servings: 4

Equipment

Stove-top
Large pan with a lid
Tongs
Manual blender
Cutting board

Ingredients

For the beef:
2 beef steaks of your choice
4 slices of prosciutto
1/2 cup pecorino
1/4 cup parmegiano reggiano
1/2 cup spinach
1 tbsp ricotta
1/4 cup pine nuts
1/4 cup bread crumbs
Salt to season

For the tomato sauce
2 tbsp olive oil
1/2 yellow onion (finely chopped)
400g chopped tomato
1 tbsp tomato puree
Pinch of salt
Pinch of sugar
Splash of red wine
Handful of fresh basil

For the Coating:
1 cup cornflakes, coarsely crushed
1/4 tsp turmeric
1/4 tsp red chilli flakes

Extras:
Parchment paper
Cocktail sticks or butchers string to hold the rolls together

How to make it

Take each steak one at a time and bash between two pieces of parchment paper to form very thin rectangular steaks. Season both sides of each steak and then set aside.

Using your manual blender, blitz up the spinach and all the cheeses to form a thick spreadable paste.

Take one steak at a time and spread over the cheesy paste followed by a layer of prosciutto, a sprinkle of breadcrumbs, and a sprinkle of pine nuts.

Start at the narrowest end and tightly roll the steak. When you get to the end, tuck in the sides to prevent the mixture from leaking out. Use cocktail sticks to pin the roll into shape or use butcher's string to tie it up.

Heat your pan over medium heat and add olive oil and the chopped onion. When the onion is soft and fragrant, add the beef. You only need to brown the sides, so flash the steaks until seared all over. When seared, pour the splash of wine over the beef and wait 2 minutes for the wine to evaporate.

Add the full can of tomatoes, the tomato purée, a generous pinch of salt, and a generous pinch of sugar. Give it a good mix and reduce the heat to very low. Place the lid on the pan but leave slightly ajar to let some steam out and cook for 45 minutes.

Make sure the sauce is gently simmering and not boiling, and give it a stir every now and then. Ten minutes before it's ready, add a big handful of basil to the sauce.

When the sauce is thick and tastes strongly of tomato, it is ready.

Remove the pins/string and slice the Braciole.

Serve with anything you like: pasta, veg... it's AMAZING with mash!

Pizza Fritte

Imagine crispy golden pizza parcels filled with tomato, melty mozzarella, and a zing of Parmesan. These irresistible bites are perfect for vanlife feasts–simple ingredients, minimal equipment, and pure joy in every mouthful. It's the kids favourite!

Prep: 10 minutes(plus 1 hour for dough proving), Cook: 10-12 mins
Servings: 6 Frittas

Equipment

Large, sturdy frying pan
Medium bowl
Clean, damp tea towel
Large slotted spoon or tongs
Paper towels for draining
Measuring cups and spoons

Ingredients

1/2 batch Neapolitan pizza dough (use the Vanlife Eats recipe, halved)
1/2 cup (50g) Parmesan cheese, finely grated
1 cup (250g) ricotta cheese
200g mozzarella cheese, torn into small pieces
1/2 bunch (15g) fresh basil leaves
1 litre vegetable oil, for frying
1 cup tinned tomatoes (finely chopped)
Extra Tipo 00 flour, for dusting

How to make it

Prepare the Dough
Prove the pizza dough for 1 hour. Divide the dough into 6 equal balls on a flour-dusted surface. Lightly dust the balls with flour, cover them with a damp tea towel, and let them rest for 10 minutes.

Make the Filling
In a medium bowl, mix the grated Parmesan with the ricotta until smooth. Set aside.

Assemble the Fritte
Roll out each dough ball into a 15cm round using your fingers or a rolling pin. Place a dollop of tomato and a heaped spoonful of the ricotta mixture in the center, add a few torn pieces of mozzarella, season lightly, and top with a couple of basil leaves. Fold the dough over the filling to form a half-moon shape, pressing the edges to seal. Twist and tuck the dough if needed to prevent leaks.

Heat the Oil
In a sturdy frying pan, heat the vegetable oil over medium-high heat. Test the oil with a small cube of potato–when it turns golden and rises to the surface, the oil is ready.

Fry the Fritte
Working in batches, carefully lower two filled dough parcels into the hot oil. Fry for 1½ minutes on each side, or until golden brown and crispy. Remove with a slotted spoon and drain on paper towels. Allow the oil to return to temperature between batches.

Serve
Arrange the fritte on a plate, sprinkle with fresh basil leaves, and enjoy while hot.

Cheese & Onion Polenta Mash

Say goodbye to boring side dishes with this super easy velvety polenta mash. Creamy, cheesy and kissed with a touch of spring onion. It's a great alternative to mash potato!

Prep: 5 minutes, Cook: 10 mins Servings: 2

Equipment

Medium saucepan
Whisk
Chopping board and knife
Measuring cups and spoons

Ingredients

1/2 cup (85g) quick-cook polenta
1 1/2 cups (375ml) water
1/2 cup (125ml) whole milk
3/4 cup (75g) sharp cheddar cheese, grated
2 spring onions, finely sliced
2 tbsp (30g) butter
Salt and black pepper, to taste

How to make it

Heat the Liquid
In a medium saucepan, bring the water and milk to a gentle simmer over medium heat. Season lightly with a pinch of salt.

Cook the Polenta
Gradually whisk in the polenta to avoid lumps. Reduce the heat to low and continue whisking for 3-4 minutes until the polenta thickens to a creamy consistency.

Add the Good Stuff
Stir in the butter and grated cheddar cheese until melted and fully combined. Taste and adjust seasoning with salt and a touch of black pepper.

Finish with Spring Onions
Fold in the sliced spring onions for a fresh pop of flavor.

Serve Hot
Dish it up immediately as a cozy side or even a topping on your Tex Mex Chilli!

French Toast

Breakfast? Pudding? Brunch? Heck, I'd even eat it for lunch! This is a modern French classic, but I've sweetened it up to make it sweeter and more cake-like. You'll love it! Guaranteed!

Prep: 5 minutes, Cook: 10 mins Servings: 2

Equipment

Medium mixing bowl
Fork or whisk
Shallow dish (like a pie pan)
Nonstick skillet or griddle
Spatula

Ingredients

2 large eggs
100 ml (about ⅓ cup + 1 tbsp) milk
½ tsp vanilla extract
¼ tsp ground cinnamon
A pinch of sea salt
1 tbsp butter
4 thick slices of brioche bread
Maple syrup or honey
Powdered sugar, for topping

How to make it

Make the Egg Mixture
In a medium mixing bowl, whisk together the eggs, milk, vanilla, cinnamon, and a pinch of sea salt until smooth. Pour the mixture into a shallow dish for easy dipping.

Heat the Skillet
Place a nonstick skillet or griddle over medium heat. Add a small knob of butter or a splash of oil, allowing it to melt and coat the surface.

Dip and Cook
Take a slice of bread and dip it into the egg mixture, turning to coat both sides evenly. Let any excess drip back into the dish, then transfer the bread to the heated skillet.

Cook each slice for about 2 minutes per side, or until golden brown. If your bread browns too quickly, lower the heat to avoid burning. Work in batches if needed, greasing the skillet lightly between rounds.

Serve and Enjoy
Stack your golden French toast onto plates, drizzle generously with maple syrup, or honey and dust with powdered sugar. Top with fresh fruit if you've got it, and dig in.

Garlicky Camembert Chicken

We all love a garlicky kiss right? Well this is the perfect date night meal. It is rich and indulgent yet so easy to throw together.

Prep: 10 minutes, Cook: 20 mins Servings: 2

Equipment

Large frying pan
Knife and cutting board
Wooden spoon or spatula

Ingredients

1 ½ tbsp olive oil
2 large chicken breasts (cut into four medallions)
1 tbsp unsalted butter
½ tsp dried thyme
Salt and black pepper, to taste
4 slices of bacon (cut into small pieces)
2 cloves garlic, minced
½ cup (120 ml) dry white wine
1 tsp Dijon mustard
1 ½ cups (375 ml) heavy cream
100 g (about half a wheel) Camembert cheese, diced into chunks
¼ tsp ground nutmeg
Fresh parsley, chopped, for garnish

Suggested Sides
Buttered tagliatelle or fettuccine
Creamy mashed potatoes
Wilted spinach or steamed green beans

How to make it

Prepare and Cook the Chicken
Slice each chicken breast at an angle to create four medallions. Season both sides with salt, pepper, and a sprinkle of dried thyme. Heat the olive oil and butter in a large frying pan over medium heat.

Once sizzling, add the chicken medallions and cook for 4-5 minutes on each side until golden and cooked through. Remove from the pan, loosely cover with foil, and set aside.

Start the Sauce
In the same pan (don't wash it–you want all those tasty bits!), add the bacon and cook for 2 minutes. Lower the heat and toss in the garlic. Sauté for about 30 seconds until fragrant.

Pour in the white wine, scrape the pan with your spoon to deglaze, and let it reduce by half. Stir in the Dijon mustard for a tangy kick.

Add the Cream and Cheese
Stir in the heavy cream, followed by the Camembert chunks and a pinch of nutmeg. Gently heat the mixture, stirring, until the cheese melts into a luscious, smooth sauce. Adjust with salt and pepper as needed.

Return the Chicken
Return the chicken medallions (plus any juices) to the pan, nestling them into the sauce. Simmer gently for 2-3 minutes to warm through and let those flavors mingle.

Plate and Serve
Plate the chicken medallions and ladle over the creamy sauce, and garnish with fresh parsley. Pair with your choice of sides for a complete meal.

Leftover sauce is pure gold – stash it for dipping crusty bread for tomorrow's lunch.

Mac n'Cheese Balls

Golden, gooey, and gloriously cheesy–these macaroni cheese balls are the ultimate comfort food treat. Whether you're parked by the beach or deep in the woods, this snack will make everything feel like a gourmet picnic.

Prep: 10 minutes (plus chilling time), Cook: 10 mins Servings: 2-4

Equipment

Mixing bowl
Baking tray
Frying pan
Slotted spoon

Ingredients

2 cups (about 400 g) leftover macaroni and cheese (see page 113)
1 egg, beaten (for mixing)
1 egg, beaten (for coating)
Breadcrumbs, as needed
Oil, for frying

How to make it

Prep the Mac & Cheese
Place your leftover macaroni and cheese in a mixing bowl. If it's too dry, stir in a beaten egg to help bind the mixture. Mix well until it holds together.

Shape the Balls
Scoop portions of the mixture and roll them into golf ball-sized spheres. If the mixture feels sticky, lightly wet your hands to shape the balls more easily.
Arrange the balls on a tray and refrigerate for 1 hour to firm up.

Bread the Balls
Dip each ball into the beaten egg, then roll in breadcrumbs to coat evenly.

Fry Until Golden
Heat a shallow layer of oil in a frying pan over medium heat.
Fry the balls in batches, turning occasionally, until they're golden brown and crispy on all sides. Use a slotted spoon to transfer them to a paper towel-lined plate.

Serve and Enjoy
Enjoy these crispy mac and cheese balls with your favourite sauce–whether it's leftover ragu or dare I say it... some simple ketchup!

Paella Skewers

Juicy prawns, tender chicken, and smoky chorizo - all the flavours of a Spanish Paella but loaded up on a skewer and served on a bed of crispy spicy rice- yep you want a burnt bottom!

Prep: 15 minutes, Cook: 20 mins Servings: 2

Equipment

Stove
Large frying pan (with a lid, optional)
Skewers (metal or soaked wooden ones)
Mixing bowls

Ingredients

For the Skewers
100g chicken breast, cut into bite-sized pieces
75g raw king prawns, peeled and deveined
75g chorizo, sliced into chunks
1 clove garlic, minced
1 tbsp olive oil
1 tsp smoked paprika
1/2 tsp dried oregano
Salt and pepper, to taste

For the Rice
1/2 cup basmati rice
1/2 red onion, finely diced
1/2 green bell pepper, chopped
1/2 tsp turmeric
1/2 tsp smoked paprika
1/2 tsp chilli flakes
1 tbsp olive oil
1 cup chicken or vegetable stock
Salt, to taste

Optional Garnish
Lemon wedges
Fresh parsley, chopped

How to make it

Marinate the Skewers
In a bowl, toss the chicken, prawns, and chorizo with olive oil, garlic, smoked paprika, oregano, salt, and pepper. Thread the pieces onto skewers in any order you fancy. Set aside.

Prepare the Rice Base
Heat olive oil in a large frying pan over medium heat. Sauté the onion and green pepper until softened. Stir in the turmeric, smoked paprika, and chilli flakes. Add the rice and toss to coat it in the spices.

Cook the Rice
Pour in the stock, bring it to a boil, then reduce the heat to low. Cover the pan and simmer until the liquid is absorbed (about 15 minutes). Remove the lid for the last few minutes and let the bottom of the rice crisp up slightly for that authentic paella-style crunch.

Cook the Skewers
Heat another pan over medium-high heat. Cook the skewers for about 2-3 minutes on each side, or until the chicken is cooked through and the prawns turn pink.

Assemble and Serve
Spoon the crispy spicy rice onto plates and top with the skewers. Garnish with fresh parsley and a squeeze of lemon for a final zing.

Creamy Potato Pierogies

Pierogies are the ultimate comfort food. Imagine biting into tender dumplings filled with a creamy, cheesy potato mixture. They're simple, satisfying, and surprisingly adaptable–even in a van kitchen!

Prep: 30 minutes, Cook: 20 mins Servings: Aprox 12 Pierogies

Equipment

Medium mixing bowl
Rolling pin
Medium saucepan
Frying pan
Slotted spoon
Fork or pastry cutter

Ingredients

For the Dough
1 ½ cups (190g) all-purpose flour, plus extra for dusting
½ tsp salt
1 large egg
¼ cup (60ml) sour cream
2 tbsp (30ml) butter, melted

For the Filling
2 medium potatoes (about 250g), peeled and diced
1 small onion, finely chopped
1 tbsp (15g) butter
½ cup (50g) shredded cheddar cheese
Salt and black pepper, to taste

For Cooking
Butter or oil, for frying

How to make it

Make the Dough
In a medium bowl, mix the flour and salt. Add the egg, sour cream, and melted butter. Stir until the dough comes together. Cover with a damp cloth and let rest for 15 minutes.

Prepare the Filling
Bring a saucepan of salted water to a boil, then toss in the diced potatoes. Simmer until tender, about 10-12 minutes.

While the potatoes cook, melt 1 tablespoon of butter in a pan over medium heat. Add the chopped onion and sauté until soft and golden.

Mash the cooked potatoes in a bowl, then stir in the sautéed onions and shredded cheddar. Season to taste with salt and black pepper. Set aside to cool.

Shape the Pierogies
Seperate the dough into two balls. Roll out the dough on a floured surface to about 2mm thick. Use a glass or cutter to cut out 3-inch circles.
Spoon a small amount of filling onto the centre of each circle. Fold the dough over the filling to form a half-moon shape. Press the edges firmly with a fork to seal.

Cook the Pierogies
Bring a large pot of salted water to a gentle boil. Drop in the pierogies in batches, stirring to prevent sticking. Cook until they float to the surface, about 3-4 minutes.

Heat butter or oil in a frying pan over medium heat. Add the boiled pierogies and flash fry until golden and crisp on both sides.

Serve and Enjoy
Serve your pierogies hot with a dollop of sour cream.

Swedish Supermarket Meatballs

Apart from Nonna's meatballs, these are everybody's favourite and often an excuse to go and buy some flat-pack furniture, huh! This recipe is for the iconic juicy balls in a rich Swedish sauce.

Prep: 10 minutes, Cook: 30 mins Servings: 2

Equipment

Large mixing bowl
Frying pan
Small saucepan
Whisk
Plate for resting meatballs

Ingredients

For the Meatballs
100g breadcrumbs
1 small onion, finely chopped
750g mixed beef & pork mince
5 tbsp whole milk
1 garlic clove, minced
1 egg
Generous salt & pepper
Oil, for frying

For the Cream Sauce
40g butter
40g plain flour
300ml beef stock
150ml thick double cream
2 tsp soy sauce
1 tsp Dijon mustard

How to make it

Make the Meatballs
In a bowl, mix the breadcrumbs and milk–this keeps the meatballs soft and juicy.

Add the minced beef and pork, chopped onion, garlic, egg, salt, and pepper. Get your hands in there and mix everything together until well combined.

Roll the mixture into small, bite-sized balls and place them on a plate. Cover and pop them in the fridge for 2 hours–this stops them from falling apart when cooking.

Cook the Meatballs
Heat a frying pan over medium heat with a little oil. Once hot, add the meatballs in batches and brown them on all sides.
Once they're golden, reduce the heat to low, cover the pan, and let them cook through for another 10-15 minutes. If they start to stick, add a splash of water.

Make the Sauce
In a small saucepan, melt the butter over medium heat. Stir in the flour and cook for 1-2 minutes, whisking constantly.
Gradually pour in the beef stock, whisking all the while to prevent lumps.
Stir in the double cream, soy sauce, and mustard. Let it bubble gently until thick and silky.

Serve & Enjoy
Spoon that glorious sauce over the meatballs and serve with mashed potatoes, crusty bread, or whatever carb-based companion you fancy. Kinda should be mash though!

Swedish Meatball Sliders

Both kids and adults are sure to delight in this innovative twist on the classic burger. Small yet powerful, these meatball sliders are simply the best! The creamy sauce seeps into the bun, creating a rich flavor that will have you savouring every delicious bite.

Prep: 5 minutes, Cook: 10 mins Servings: 4 Sliders

Equipment

Frying pan
Small saucepan
Spatula
Knife & cutting board

Ingredients

4 small bread rolls
4 cooked meatballs (see page 127)
A few spinach leaves (or lettuce)
2 tbsp Swedish lingonberry sauce (or cranberry sauce)

How to make it

Slice the bread rolls in half and lightly toast them in a dry pan.

Place a few spinach leaves on the bottom half of each roll.

Add a warm meatball with a spoonful of sauce.

Top with a little lingonberry (or cranberry) sauce for that sweet contrast.

Pop the other half of the roll on top and serve immediately.

Lamb Koftas With Yoghurt Dip

Middle Eastern flavours, minimal fuss, and cooked right on your campervan stovetop. Juicy lamb koftas wrapped in soft van-made flatbreads and dipped in a fresh yoghurt dip.

Prep: 15 minutes, Cook: 15 mins Servings: 2

Equipment

Mixing bowl
Box grater
Skewers (or just shape into patties!)
Frying pan or griddle
Tongs

Ingredients

For the Koftas
250g lamb mince
1 garlic clove, crushed
1/2 small onion, grated
Pinch of salt and pepper
1 tbsp fresh coriander, chopped
1/2 tsp cayenne pepper (adjust to taste)
1 tsp cumin
1 tsp paprika
1 tsp ground coriander
¾ tsp ground cinnamon
2 tbsp breadcrumbs (preferably panko)

For the Yoghurt Dressing
1/2 cup Greek yoghurt
1/2 tbsp extra virgin olive oil
1/2 tbsp lemon juice
1/2 tsp cumin
1 garlic clove, crushed
Pinch of salt and black pepper

How to make it

Make the Yoghurt Dressing
In a small bowl, mix together the yoghurt, olive oil, lemon juice, cumin, garlic, salt, and black pepper.
Pop it in the fridge while you cook–it tastes even better once the flavours meld.

Prepare the Koftas
In a mixing bowl, grate the onion, then add the lamb mince, garlic, salt, pepper, coriander, cayenne, cumin, paprika, cinnamon, breadcrumbs, and ground coriander.

Using your hands, mix everything until well combined. Try not to overwork the meat–it keeps them tender.

With damp hands, divide the mixture into 4 equal portions and shape them around skewers (or into small oval patties if you don't have skewers).

Cook the Koftas
Heat a frying pan or griddle over medium-high heat and drizzle with a little oil.
Cook the koftas for about 5-6 minutes, turning occasionally, until browned and cooked through.

Assemble & Serve
Warm the flatbreads in the pan or over the flame for a few seconds.

Load them up with shredded lettuce, tomato, and onion slices, then top with the koftas.

Drizzle generously with the yoghurt dressing and scatter over fresh coriander if using.
Wrap it up, take a big bite, and enjoy!

Mark's Legendary Mac n' Cheese

Rich decadent creamy mac and cheese with the perfect combination of crunch to munch. This one is special to me. The secret is definitely the combination and ratio of cheese!

Prep: 5 minutes, Cook: 15 mins Servings: 2

Equipment

Large saucepan
Frying pan
Whisk
Wooden spoon
Small bowl

Ingredients

1½ cups macaroni
¼ cup pancetta, diced
2 tbsp breadcrumbs
1 tbsp unsalted butter
1 tbsp plain flour
1 cup whole milk
½ cup pecorino, finely grated
¼ cup parmesan, finely grated
½ tsp paprika
A pinch of nutmeg
Salt & black pepper, to taste

How to make it

Crunch Time
In a frying pan over medium heat, cook the pancetta until the fat renders and it starts to crisp up. Toss in the breadcrumbs and stir until golden and crunchy. Tip into a bowl and set aside.

Make The Cheese Sauce
In the same pan, melt the butter, then stir in the flour to make a roux. Cook it for a minute or two until it looks like wet sand. Take it off the heat, add a splash of milk, and whisk until smooth. Put it back on the heat and add the rest of the milk bit by bit, whisking in between, until you have a smooth, silky, runny sauce.

Season & Cheese It Up
Stir in the paprika, nutmeg, salt, and black pepper. Then, add the pecorino and parmesan, stirring until fully melted.

Macaroni Meets Cheese
Cook the macaroni in a separate pan of boiling salted water until just al dente. Drain and add it straight into the cheesy sauce, stirring to coat everything in that glorious, silky goodness.

Serve
Serve into bowls and sprinkle over the crispy pancetta and breadcrumbs for that perfect crunch!

Smoky Cavolo Nero with Chorizo & Preserved Lemon

A quick, punchy one-pan wonder for vanlife cooking. Earthy cavolo nero meets smoky, spicy chorizo, and a hit of zesty preserved lemon. Minimal effort, max flavour and super nutritious.

Prep: 5 minutes, Cook: 10 mins Servings: 2

Equipment

Frying pan (big enough to fit all the greens)
Sharp knife
Chopping board
Wooden spoon

Ingredients

200g cavolo nero (or kale), stems removed, leaves roughly chopped
100g chorizo, cut into small chunks
1 small garlic clove, finely chopped
1/2 cup cannellini beans
1/2 preserved lemon, finely diced (or zest of ½ lemon if you're improvising)
2 tbsp soured cream
1 tbsp olive oil
1 tbsp water
1/2 tsp smoked paprika
Pinch of chilli flakes (optional, for a little extra heat)
Salt & black pepper, to taste

How to make it

Cook the Chorizo & Garlic

Heat the olive oil in a large pan over medium-high heat. Once hot, add the chorizo and fry for 3-4 minutes, stirring occasionally, until browned and slightly crispy. Toss in the garlic and cook for about a minute, just until it starts to turn golden. Stir in the paprika, then use a slotted spoon to transfer the chorizo and garlic to a small bowl.

Wilt the Cavolo Nero

Add the cavolo nero to the same pan in batches, stirring to coat in the infused oil. Once all the greens are in, add the water, season with salt and a generous amount of black pepper, then cover and let it steam for 3 minutes. Give it a stir once or twice to help it soften. Remove the lid and add the cannellini beans and continue cooking for another 5-6 minutes, stirring frequently, until the liquid evaporates and the leaves are tender but still slightly crisp at the edges.

Combine & Serve

Return the chorizo and garlic to the pan, then stir in the preserved lemon and/or lemon juice. Remove from the heat and fold in the soured cream. Mix well, then serve immediately–either plated up for two or straight from the pan.

Easy French Onion Soup

I've always thought this dish is seriously underrated. It's AMAZING! The rich flavours of the caramelised onions combined with the creaminess of the cheese are just perfect, and the best part? You get to scoop it up with bread...YES PLEASE!

Prep: 10 minutes, Cook: 45 mins Servings: 2

Equipment

Large saucepan
Wooden spoon
Small knife
Cheese grater
Ladle
Two bowls

Ingredients

2 large yellow onions, thinly sliced
1½ tbsp unsalted butter
1½ cups vegetable stock
½ cup dry white wine (or extra stock)
1 tsp balsamic vinegar
1 small garlic clove, minced
1 tsp fresh thyme (or ½ tsp dried)
1 bay leaf
½ tsp salt, plus more to taste
¼ tsp black pepper
2 small slices of baguette (or any crusty bread)
½ cup grated Gruyère cheese (or any melty cheese you have)
1 spring onion

How to make it

Caramelise the Onions
Melt the butter in a saucepan over low heat. Add the onions and a pinch of salt. Cook slowly, stirring occasionally, for 30-35 minutes, until they're soft, deep golden brown, and jammy. If they start sticking, add a splash of water and scrape up the goodness.

Build the Flavour
Toss in the garlic, thyme, and bay leaf. Stir for a minute until fragrant, then pour in the wine (or extra stock) and let it simmer for a few minutes to cook off the sharpness. Add the vegetable stock, balsamic vinegar, black pepper, and another pinch of salt. Simmer for 10 minutes.

Toast the Bread
While the soup is simmering, toast the baguette slices in a dry pan over medium heat until crisp and golden.

Cheese It Up
Ladle the soup into bowls. Place a toasted baguette slice on top of each and pile on the grated cheese. Cover the bowls with a lid or foil for a minute to help the cheese melt (or just let the heat of the soup do its thing).

Garnish and Dig In!
Garnish with the spring onion. Serve hot, preferably with a spoon big enough to scoop up those glorious cheesy, oniony bites.

Easy Tomato Chutney

This no-fuss, flavour-packed chutney is a van fridge essential. It's tangy, a little sweet, and has just the right kick of heat – perfect for spooning over toasties, stirring into pasta, or loading into a burger. Plus, it's all made in one pan!

Prep: 2 minutes, Cook: 0 mins Servings: 1 Cup

Equipment

Manual blender
Chopping board & knife
Medium saucepan
Wooden spoon

Ingredients

4 large tomatoes
1 small red onion
2 tbsp soft brown sugar
1 tbsp apple cider vinegar
½ tsp chilli flakes (adjust to taste)
Pinch of cinnamon
Pinch of salt

How to make it

Roughly chop the tomatoes and onion, then blend them together until smooth using your manual blender.

Pour the mixture into a saucepan over medium heat.

Stir in the sugar, vinegar, chilli flakes, cinnamon, and a pinch of salt.

Let it simmer, stirring occasionally, until it thickens into a rich, jammy chutney–around 10-15 minutes.

Taste and adjust seasoning if needed. Let cool slightly before serving.

Best Ever Lamb Burgers with a Spicy Chutney

Juicy, herby, and packed with flavour–these lamb burgers are a real favourite. They're easy to throw together, cook in one pan, and taste ridiculously good with a dollop of homemade tomato chutney. No fancy skills required, just a bit of mixing, shaping, and sizzling!

Prep: 5 minutes, Cook: 10 mins Servings: 2

Equipment

Mixing bowl
Chopping board & knife
Plate or tray
Frying pan
Spatula

Ingredients

200g lamb mince
1 small red onion, finely chopped
1 tbsp fresh coriander, chopped
2 tbsp breadcrumbs
1 tbsp grated parmesan
1 egg
1 tbsp olive oil
1 tbsp plain flour (for shaping)
Pinch of salt & black pepper
Salad leaves, to serve
Optional: Tangy Tomato Chutney (see page 139)

How to make it

In a mixing bowl, combine the lamb mince, chopped onion, coriander, breadcrumbs, parmesan, and egg.

Season with salt and black pepper.

Mix everything together with your hands until well combined.

Lightly dust a surface with flour, then shape the mixture into two burger patties.

Heat the olive oil in a frying pan over medium heat.

Cook the burgers for about 4-5 minutes per side, until golden brown and cooked through.

Serve hot with salad leaves and a generous spoonful of tangy tomato chutney.

Gnocchi Bolognese

A hearty, comforting one-pan wonder, perfect for tiny kitchen cooking. Fluffy gnocchi soak up a rich, meaty sauce packed with deep, savoury flavours.

Prep: 10 minutes, Cook: 35 mins Servings: 2

Equipment

Large frying pan
Wooden spoon
Chopping board & knife

Ingredients

400g potato gnocchi
500g ground beef
1 small carrot, finely chopped
1 small celery stick, finely chopped
1 cup onion, chopped
2 tbsp olive oil
2 tbsp tomato puree
400g chopped tomatoes
1 cup chicken stock (made with a stock cube + hot water)
1 splash of red or white wine
1 splash of milk
½ tbsp oregano
2 bay leaves
½ tbsp sugar
Fresh basil leaves, to serve
1 cup pecorino cheese, grated
Salt & black pepper, to taste

How to make it

Heat the olive oil in a large frying pan over medium heat. Throw in the carrot, celery, and onion, and cook until soft and fragrant–about 5 minutes.

Add the ground beef and cook until browned all over, breaking it up with a spoon as you go.

Splash in the wine and let it bubble away for a minute, scraping up any stuck bits from the bottom of the pan (that's where the flavour is hiding).

Stir in the chopped tomatoes, tomato puree, salt, and sugar. Give it a good mix.

Pour in the chicken stock, chuck in the bay leaves and oregano, and stir. Let it simmer uncovered for about 20 minutes, stirring occasionally, until the sauce thickens and deepens in flavour.

Stir in the splash of milk–it rounds out the sauce beautifully.

Add the gnocchi into the pan, stirring well to coat them in the sauce. Let them cook for 5 minutes, soaking up all that goodness.

Grate in the pecorino and stir it through until melty and delicious.

Fish out the bay leaves, scatter over fresh basil, and dig in.

Spinach Frittata

I love making this in the van! It's so tasty and everyone I make it for goes in for seconds! It's healthy, keto-friendly, and ridiculously high in protein. Most importantly, it's incredibly delicious!

Prep: 5 minutes, Cook: 10 mins Servings: 2

Equipment

Frying pan (bonus points if it's a RidgeMonkey for easy flipping)
Bowl
Whisk or fork
Knife & chopping board (if your spinach needs a chop)

Ingredients

3 eggs
1 handful fresh spinach (or frozen, thawed & squeezed dry)
20g Parmesan cheese, grated
¼ tsp nutmeg
Salt & black pepper, to taste

How to make it

Bring a small pot of water to a boil and quickly blanch the spinach for about 2 minutes. Drain, squeeze out excess liquid (seriously, get all that water out), and roughly chop.

In a bowl, lightly whisk the eggs. Stir in the spinach, nutmeg, salt, and pepper. Grate in the Parmesan and mix well.

Heat a pan over medium heat and drizzle in a little oil or butter. Pour in the egg mixture and let it cook undisturbed until the edges start to set.

Here's the tricky bit–flipping. If you're using a RidgeMonkey, just close it and flip. Otherwise, slide the frittata onto a plate, place the pan over it, and flip it back in. Cook the other side until lightly golden.

Serve hot, straight from the pan or on a plate.

Camembert Cob

Bread and cheese is everyone's guilty pleasure. This recipe is such a crowd-pleaser, and everyone will eagerly dig in to enjoy this indulgent, cheesy delight!

Prep: 5 minutes, Cook: 5 mins Servings: 4+

Equipment

You need a RidgeMonkey XL sandwich toaster for this one!

Alternatively you need a large pan and a weighted pan that will sit inside.

Ingredients

1 cob loaf that is the perfect size for your RidgeMonkey pan
1 camembert cheese
1/2 cup sundried tomatoes
Fresh rosemary sprigs

How to make it

Cut a hole in the top of your cob so you have a lid and scoop out all of the bread. Save the bread; you never know when you may need it for breadcrumbs.

Place the camembert in the cut-out hole and slice some slits in the cheese.

Wedge some sun-dried tomatoes and rosemary into the slits in the cheese.

Place the lid back on the cob.

Place the cob in the pan and close the lid (or place a weighted pan on top). Squash the bread!

Cook for 2-3 minutes on the hob, flipping halfway through. If you are using the weighted pan method, then you need to physically remove the cob and turn it over (start lid side down).

Remove when toasted on the top and bottom and place in the center of your table and pick and dip away!

Tuscan Tomato Soup

This rustic Italian tomato and bread soup is comfort in a bowl. Simple, hearty, and perfect for vanlife, it turns basic ingredients into a thick, rich dish with minimal effort. Plus, it's a great way to use up stale bread

Prep: 5 minutes, Cook: 25 mins Servings: 4+

Equipment

Large saucepan
Wooden spoon
Ladle
Knife & chopping board

Ingredients

1 ½ cups (100g) rustic bread, torn into chunks (fresh or stale)
1 ½ cups (350ml) warm vegetable stock (or more as needed)
1 tbsp extra-virgin olive oil, plus extra for serving
1 garlic clove, thinly sliced
¼ tsp red pepper flakes
½ medium onion, finely chopped (about ¼ cup)
1 (400g) can chopped tomatoes,
1 sprig fresh basil, plus extra leaves for garnish
Salt and black pepper, to taste

How to make it

Heat the olive oil in a large saucepan over medium heat. Add the garlic and red pepper flakes, stirring until the garlic just starts to turn golden. Toss in the chopped onion and cook for about 5 minutes, until softened.

Pour in the crushed tomatoes (and all their juices), chuck in the basil sprig, and bring everything to a gentle simmer.

Stir in the bread chunks, then gradually ladle in the warm vegetable stock. Give it a good stir so the bread starts soaking up all the rich tomato goodness. Let it simmer, stirring occasionally, until the bread breaks down into a thick, porridge-like consistency–this takes about 20-25 minutes. Add more stock if it gets too thick.

Fish out the basil sprig and season with salt and black pepper. Spoon the soup into bowls, drizzle generously with extra olive oil, and top with fresh basil leaves.

Risotto Primavera

This Risotto Primavera, inspired by Italian springtime, is a fresh and creamy dish packed with seasonal vegetables. Made on a stovetop in one pot, it's perfect for those looking to cook something hearty yet light whilst embracing simplicity.

Prep: 15 minutes, Cook: 35 mins Servings: 2

Equipment

Medium saucepan or pot
Wooden spoon
Knife and chopping board

Ingredients

⅔ cup (100g) fresh or frozen peas
⅔ cup (100g) asparagus, chopped into bite-sized pieces
¾ cup (100g) courgettes, sliced
⅔ cup (100g) French beans, trimmed
1 tbsp olive oil
½ large onion, finely chopped
⅔ cup (125g) risotto rice
1½ cups (350ml) warm vegetable or chicken stock
2 tbsp white wine
1 tbsp fresh parsley, chopped
½ tbsp fresh thyme leaves
2 tbsp (40g) butter
½ cup (50g) grated Parmesan cheese, plus extra to serve
Salt and pepper, to taste

How to make it

Pod the peas (if fresh), chop the asparagus and courgettes, and trim the beans. Set aside.

Bring a small saucepan of salted water to a boil. Add the prepared vegetables and blanch for 1 minute. Drain and set aside.

Heat the olive oil in a medium saucepan over a medium heat. Add the chopped onion and sauté gently for 8-10 minutes until soft.

Add the risotto rice to the pan and stir for 2 minutes to coat the grains in the oil. Add the wine and wait for it to dissolve. Lower the heat slightly and add a ladleful of the warm stock, stirring until absorbed. Continue adding stock, one ladle at a time, until the rice is nearly cooked (about 15-18 minutes).

Stir in the parsley, and thyme along with the last ladle of stock. Simmer for another 5 minutes until the rice is tender but slightly al dente.

Add the butter, Parmesan cheese, and blanched vegetables. Stir gently until the vegetables are heated through and the risotto is creamy. Season with salt and pepper to taste. Serve warm with extra Parmesan on top.

Fully Loaded Paella

There are so many ways to make a paella and it's a discussion on what's truly authentic. Sometimes it just doesn't matter if it tastes good, right? This one is my favourite as it is fully loaded with chicken, prawn, and chorizo. Yessss!

Prep: 10 minutes, Cook: 30 mins Servings: 2

Equipment

Large frying pan or deep skillet (with a lid)
Sharp knife
Chopping board
Wooden spoon
Measuring cups & spoons

Ingredients

1/2 cup (100g) paella rice (or arborio rice)
1/2 a small onion, finely chopped
1/2 red bell pepper, chopped
1 garlic clove, minced
1 small chicken thigh, chopped into bite-sized pieces
50g chorizo, sliced
6 raw prawns, peeled & deveined
1 tbsp tomato paste
1/2 tsp smoked paprika
1/4 tsp saffron threads (optional, but worth it)
1 1/4 cups (300ml) chicken stock
1 tbsp olive oil
Salt & black pepper, to taste
A handful of frozen peas
Lemon wedges, for serving
Fresh parsley, chopped (optional)

How to make it

Heat the olive oil in your pan over medium heat. Toss in the chorizo and cook for 2-3 minutes until it starts releasing its spicy, smoky oils. Add the chicken pieces and cook for another 5 minutes until golden on the outside.

Stir in the onion, garlic, and bell pepper. Cook for 3-4 minutes until softened. Add the smoked paprika and saffron, giving everything a quick mix so those spices wake up.

Stir in the rice, making sure each grain gets coated in the lovely, flavoured oil. Then add the tomato paste and stock, stirring gently. Season with salt and black pepper.

Lower the heat to a gentle simmer and let it do its thing for 15-18 minutes. Resist the urge to stir–this is what gives paella its signature crispy bottom layer.

Scatter the prawns and peas over the top in the last 5 minutes of cooking. Pop the lid on and let the prawns turn pink and juicy.

Take the pan off the heat and let it rest for a couple of minutes. Sprinkle over fresh parsley, squeeze over some lemon juice, and dig in straight from the pan (because washing plates is overrated).

COOKPAD

Lobster Thermidor in a Coconut Sweet Chilli Bisque

Who needs a fancy brunch when you can whip up this ridiculously good breakfast right on your stovetop? Crispy tortilla chips, creamy avocado, smoky black beans, and a perfectly fried egg.

Prep: 5 minutes, Cook: 20 mins Servings: 2

Equipment

Frying pan
Small saucepan
Knife
Chopping board
Spatula

Ingredients

1 Lobster Live if you are brave or if precooked reduce cooking time by 10 minutes
200g Coconut Milk Full Fat
1 Lemon
2 tbsp Sweet Chilli Sauce
1 tsp Cayenne Pepper
1 tbsp Parsley Fresh or Dried
1 tsp Salt
1 cup Water
1 tsp Garlic Granules
1 cup Cheddar Cheese
1 tbsp Tomato Paste Puree

How to make it

Preheat your skillet pan to a medium/high heat.

Cut your lobster in half from the top of the head to tail. Do this quickly and firmly using a large sharp knife. Afterwards cut off the arms and legs.

Place the lobster meat side down and place the other parts of the lobster in the pan around it.
Cook meat side down for 5 minutes. (3 minutes if using a pre cooked lobster) The meat should start to go golden brown.
Turn the lobster (and claws etc.) over so it is shell side down.

Pour in around the lobster the cup of water, half the tin of coconut milk, the garlic granules, tomato paste, cayenne pepper and sweet chilli sauce.

Season the lobster and bisque with salt and then squeeze half the lemon over the meat.

Bring it to the boil and then let simmer for 5 minutes
Grate the cheese over the top of the meat and sprinkle parsley over everything in the pan.

When the cheese has melted you are ready to serve it up in a bowl with a wedge of lemon.

Easy Focaccia

One of my absolute favourite breads! Drizzled with a sweet balsamic and served with fresh mozzarella and basil...oh man! Dribble!!

Overnight resting plus a further 4 hours, Cook: 45 mins Servings: 2-4

Equipment

Omnia stove-top oven (no silicone liner)
Large mixing bowl
Measuring cups & spoons
Wooden spoon or spatula
Clean kitchen towel
Clean fingers (for the essential focaccia dimples!)

No Omnia? Use your standard oven!

Ingredients

500g plain flour
1 tsp salt
1 tsp instant yeast
1 cup lukewarm water (adjust accordingly)
1 tsp honey
1/2 cup olive oil (plus extra for greasing and drizzling)
Balsamic vinegar, to drizzle

How to make it

Make the Starter (The Night Before)
In a bowl, mix the yeast, honey, lukewarm water, and 2 tablespoons of flour. Stir well until it forms a smooth, porridge-like consistency. Cover and leave overnight to activate.

Make the Dough
The next day, add the remaining flour, half a cup of water, salt, and 1 tablespoon of olive oil to the starter. Stir everything together until a shaggy dough forms. If it's too dry, add a splash more water. Knead lightly in the bowl for a minute or two until it starts to come together. It should feel soft and slightly sticky.

First Rise
Cover the bowl with a kitchen towel and let the dough rise for 2 hours, or until it has doubled in size. If you're in a warm van, this might happen faster.

Prepare the Omnia
Generously coat the inside of the Omnia pan with olive oil–this prevents sticking and gives the focaccia its golden crust.

Shape & Second Rise
Transfer the dough into the oiled Omnia, spreading it out gently with your hands. Drizzle another tablespoon of olive oil over the top and use your fingers to poke deep dimples all over the surface. Cover with a towel and let it rest for another 2 hours.

Bake on the Stovetop
Place the Omnia on low heat and bake for 45 minutes. Resist the urge to crank up the heat–slow and steady wins here! Check after 40 minutes; it should be golden brown on top and sound hollow when tapped.

Finishing Touches
Let the focaccia cool slightly, then drizzle generously with balsamic vinegar and a final splash of olive oil. Tear apart and enjoy.

Souvlaki Chicken

Souvlaki simply means meat on a skewer, but we are going to marinade these beauties for a juicy, garlicky flavour. Wrap it up in a warm pitta with cool tzatziki, and you've got yourself a vanlife feast.

Prep: 15 minutes, Cook: 10 mins Servings: 2

Equipment

Mixing bowl
Chopping board & knife
Griddle pan or frying pan
Tongs
Small bowl
Kitchen towel

Ingredients

For the Chicken Souvlaki
2 boneless chicken breasts (about 500g)
2 tbsp olive oil
Juice of ½ a lemon
1 clove garlic, minced
1 tbsp dried oregano
Salt & black pepper, to taste
4 wooden skewers (soaked in water for 10 minutes)

For the Tzatziki
½ cucumber, grated
120g Greek yoghurt
½ tbsp olive oil
½ clove garlic, minced
1 tbsp red wine vinegar
Pinch of salt & black pepper

For Serving
2 pitta breads
½ red onion, thinly sliced
1 small tomato, sliced
Lemon wedges
Extra oregano & olive oil for garnish

How to make it

Marinate the Chicken
Chop the chicken into bite-sized chunks (about 2-3 cm pieces) and place them in a bowl.

Add olive oil, lemon juice, garlic, oregano, salt, and black pepper. Mix well–yes, hands are best for this!
Cover and let it marinate in the fridge for at least 30 minutes (or as long as you can resist).

Make the Tzatziki
Sprinkle a little salt over the grated cucumber and let it sit for 10 minutes. Then, wrap it in a kitchen towel and squeeze out the excess water.

In a bowl, mix the cucumber with yoghurt, olive oil, garlic, vinegar, salt, and pepper. Stir well and pop it in the fridge –it's best served cold.

Cook the Chicken
Heat a griddle pan (or frying pan) over medium-high heat.

Thread the marinated chicken onto the soaked skewers.
Cook for about 8-10 minutes, turning occasionally, until the chicken is golden and cooked through.

Toast the Pita
Brush the pita breads lightly with olive oil and sprinkle with oregano.

Warm them in the griddle pan for about 1-2 minutes per side.

Assemble & Serve
Lay out the pitta, spread a generous scoop of tzatziki, and pile on the chicken, red onion, and tomato.

Drizzle with extra olive oil, squeeze over some lemon juice, and dig in.

Creamy One-Pan Mushroom Risotto

Rich, earthy, and ridiculously comforting, this mushroom risotto is an Italian-approved dinner that feels fancy but is secretly dead easy. No oven, no stress–just one pan!

Prep: 5 minutes, Cook: 25 mins Servings: 2

Equipment

Large frying pan or shallow saucepan
Chopping board & knife
Wooden spoon
Small bowl

Ingredients

150g risotto rice (Arborio works best)
25g dried porcini mushrooms
1 vegetable stock cube
1 tbsp olive oil
1 small onion, finely chopped
1 garlic clove, minced
125g chestnut mushrooms, roughly chopped
½ glass (85ml) white wine
15g butter
25g parmesan, grated
Handful of fresh parsley, chopped
Salt & black pepper to taste

How to make it

Prep the Mushrooms
Chuck the dried porcini mushrooms into a small bowl and cover with 500ml of boiling water. Let them soak for 20 minutes while you get everything else sorted. Once they've plumped up, drain them, but don't chuck the soaking liquid–this is pure gold for flavour. Just leave the last few spoonfuls behind to avoid any gritty bits.

Make a Mushroom Stock
Dissolve a stock cube into the mushroom soaking liquid and give the soaked porcini mushrooms a gentle squeeze to get rid of excess liquid. Chop them up finely and set aside.

Sauté the Good Stuff
Heat the olive oil in your frying pan over medium heat. Toss in the onion and garlic, and cook for about 5 minutes until soft and fragrant. Add the chestnut mushrooms and the chopped porcini, season with salt and black pepper, and let them cook down for another 8 minutes until soft and slightly golden.

Toast the Rice
Stir in the risotto rice, coating it in all that mushroomy goodness. Let it toast for a minute before pouring in the white wine. Stir until the wine evaporates completely.

The Stirring Game
Ladle in about a quarter of your mushroom stock, stirring regularly, and let the rice soak it up. Once the liquid is nearly gone, add another ladleful and repeat. Keep this going until you've used all the stock–this should take around 20 minutes. The risotto should be creamy, and the rice should be tender with a slight bite.

The Final Touches
Take the pan off the heat and stir in the butter, half the grated parmesan, and half the chopped parsley. Cover with a lid and let it sit for a few minutes to absorb any extra liquid.

Serve & Enjoy
Give it a final stir, spoon into bowls, and top with the remaining parmesan and parsley.

Spinach & Ricotta Pancake Parcels

Fluffy pancakes stuffed with creamy ricotta and spinach, smothered in a rich tomato sauce, and baked to perfection in the Omnia. This dish feels fancy but is actually ridiculously easy.

Prep: 10 minutes, Cook: 20 mins Servings: 2

Equipment

Frying pan
Manual blender
Omnia stovetop oven

Ingredients

Pancake Mix
1/8 cup cold water
2 large eggs
2 heaped tbsp self-raising flour
1 pinch salt
Filling
125g ricotta cheese
200g baby spinach
1 tsp salt
1 pinch grated nutmeg
Tomato Sauce
200g passata
1 tbsp tomato purée
1 tbsp sugar
½ tsp salt
For Cooking & Serving
2 tbsp olive oil
50g Parmigiano Reggiano

Bonus Tip
Feeling adventurous? Swap the filling for mozzarella and ham for a gooey, cheesy twist!

How to make it

Make the Pancakes
Heat 1 tbsp of olive oil in a frying pan over medium heat. In a bowl, whisk the eggs with cold water and a pinch of salt. Gradually sprinkle in the flour, whisking as you go to avoid lumps.

Pour a little batter into the centre of the pan and tilt the pan to spread it into a 6-inch circle. Fry for about 40 seconds, then flip and cook for another 20 seconds until lightly golden. Transfer to a plate and repeat until you have 6 pancakes.

Prepare the Filling
Blitz half of the spinach in your manual blender (about 4 pulls). Add the rest of the spinach and blend again. Mix in the ricotta, nutmeg, and salt, then give it another few pulls until well combined.

Assemble the Parcels
Place a heaped tablespoon of filling in the centre of each pancake, then fold them into small parcels.

Cook in the Omnia
Swap your frying pan for the Omnia and preheat it over low heat. Meanwhile, mix the passata with tomato purée, sugar, and salt.

Pour 1 tbsp olive oil and half the tomato sauce into the Omnia tin. Arrange the pancake parcels in a circle, then pour over the remaining sauce. Sprinkle with half of the Parmigiano Reggiano.

Cover and cook over very low heat for 20 minutes. The pancakes will puff up beautifully as they absorb the sauce.

Serve & Enjoy
Divide between two plates (3 parcels each) and top with the remaining Parmigiano Reggiano.

Acknowledgements & Thanks

Well, here we are–the end of the book and this cookbook wouldn't exist without the incredible people who've fuelled it–literally and figuratively.

To Sophie

Above anyone else I know Sophie understands the effort that's gone in to making this cook book and never in a million years would I have ever been able to do it without her support and encouragement. All the late nights, the conversations about food, hogging the TV remote to watch cooking shows, the mess in the van (as well as her house) and for helping me with wording and spellings. To be honest I wouldn't be able to run Vanlife Eats at all without her...I'm actually wondering if there's anything I can do without her?? She's the best and I am incredibly lucky!!

To the Vanlife Community

To every fellow van-dweller, weekend warrior, and campfire chef who's shared tips, mishaps, and genius food hacks–this book is for you. Whether you're cooking on a two-ring hob, a rickety old camping stove, or straight-up over a fire, your passion for food is inspiring.

To Family & Friends

You've endured my relentless recipe testing, sat patiently through my "wait, let me take a photo first" moments, and eaten some very questionable first attempts. Your support, feedback, and occasional brutal honesty have made these recipes better–and edible.

To Nonna & Aunty Marisa

Some people go to culinary school. I had Nonna–the best culinary school anyone could ever wish for. She taught me that cooking isn't just about food–it's about love, patience, and never letting anyone leave the table hungry. Aunty Marisa, you carried on that tradition, teaching me to cook from the heart. This book exists because of you both, and I hope it does you proud.

To Mum

Mum, you've always taught me that fresh is best and to always avoid those "ping ping" meals!. Your passion for homemade meals, and feeding people properly has shaped the way I cook today.

To My Taste-Testers & Critics

You know who you are. You took one for the team by sampling everything, from triumphs to total disasters. Your enthusiasm (or strategic avoidance) shaped every dish in this book.

To the Kids

I told you my weird food wasn't poisonous! I'm so proud of how brave you all are in trying new flavours and it fills my heart when you've said you actually enjoyed it. You can go back to chicken nuggets for a little while now!

To You–Yes, You!

If you're flipping through these pages, considering what to cook next, or planning your next van adventure, thank you for bringing this book into your kitchen-on-wheels. May your meals be easy, tasty, and not require too much washing up.
Now, get out there, keep cooking, and remember–burnt edges may just add flavour!

Get ready for book 2 everyone!!! .....gulp!

zyliss
WINNERWELL
SAVERNAKE
Vanlife
Eats
omnia

VANLIFE EATS

Vanlife Eats
www.vanlifeeats.com

VanLife Eats

BIG PICNIC

VAN
ROAST

Index